STUDY & LIVE
IN BRITAIN

Jane Woolfenden

Northcote House

First published in 1990 by Northcote House Publishers Ltd, Plymbridge House, Estover Road, Plymouth PL6 7PZ, United Kingdom.
Tel: Plymouth (0752) 705251. Fax: (0752) 777603. Telex: 45635.

British Library Cataloguing in Publication Data
Woolfenden, Jane,
  How to study and live in Britain. – (How to books).
  1. Great Britain. Higher education institutions.
  I. Title
  378'.1982

  ISBN 0-7463-0377-7

Typeset by St. George Typesetting, Redruth, Cornwall
Printed and bound by Billing & Sons Ltd, Worcester

Contents

Preface

This book is intended primarily for anyone from overseas who is planning to come to Britain to study at a British school, college, polytechnic or university. It will not only help you to make a decision about what and where to study, where to live and so on, but also, once the choice has been made, it will provide you with all the practical information you need to help you to put your plans into action.

Before making any decisions, obtain information from as many different sources as possible; for example, from friends or relatives who have studied in Britain, from written information produced by the schools and colleges and from the British Council office in your home country.

This book will also provide invaluable information on practical steps you need to take before leaving home and will help you to deal with some of the problems you may have when you arrive in Britain.

It will, of course, also deal with the rewarding and pleasurable aspects of living and studying in Britain, and help you to make the most of what Britain has to offer. Above all, this book will help you to enjoy your stay and to make the most of your time as a student in Britain.

Good luck!

1
Courses and Colleges

THE BRITISH EDUCATIONAL SYSTEM

In Britain, education is *compulsory* for anyone between the ages of 5 and 16. It is, however, available for people of all ages.

Educational institutions in Britain can be divided into two categories. There are **state maintained** institutions and **independent sector** institutions.

State maintained schools, colleges, polytechnics and universities are financed partly or wholly by the government. Independent sector institutions, which are sometimes called **private** schools and colleges, or **fee-paying** schools, are independent of government control, although they have to be registered with the government. *All* independent sector institutions charge fees. Unfortunately, some of the oldest independent sector schools are called **public schools**, which is rather confusing!

The school year
The school or college year in Britain usually begins in September or October. The year is then divided into three terms:

- **Autumn term** — September to mid-December;
- **Spring term** — January to March/April;
- **Summer term** — April to July.

If someone asks you, "When are you **breaking up**?" they mean, when does your term end?

CHOOSING A COURSE

If you are under the age of 14, you do not usually have any choice about which subjects you study at school or the type of course you will follow.

Once you have reached 13 or 14 you are allowed to make a choice about some of the subjects you take.

From the age of 16, you have a free choice, and there is a wide range of different types of courses, subjects and qualifications. The decision is yours, but it may not always be easy. A wrong choice could mean wasted time and wasted money, especially if you are a student from overseas.

Making a decision
Before choosing a course, first of all think about what you want to do when you have *finished* the course.

Ask yourself the following questions:

- Why am I taking the course?
- Is it to help me to get a job, or a better job?
- Is it because I want to go on to do further courses?
- Have I got the right qualifications to do the course?
- Will this course give me the right qualifications for the job I want, or for the next course I want to take?
- Is this the right course for my long term objectives?
- Will the qualifications I obtain be of use to me if I change my plans in the future?

It is important not to rush making your decision. If you make a mistake about your choice of course, you can sometimes change to another course in the first few weeks, but try to avoid doing this too often:

- It is not good for your academic progress.
- It can become very expensive.
- It may give the Home Office the impression that you are not a genuine student (see Chapter 4).

WHAT QUALIFICATIONS CAN I OBTAIN IN BRITAIN?

GCSE
Since 1987, the General Certificate of Secondary Education (GCSE) examinations have replaced the O level examinations. There are over 100 different subjects to choose from, but some schools offer a wider choice than others.

Courses leading to GCSE exams normally last for two years. Most students take their GCSE exams when they are 15 or 16, but there is no age limit.

The main feature of the new GCSE exams is that you are assessed on work and projects which you have completed during the course (**continuous assessment**), as well as by a final written exam which usually takes place in June. For each exam you pass, you will be awarded a **grade**; A,B,C,D,E,F or G.

GCSE examinations are prepared and marked by six **examining groups** in England, Northern Ireland and Wales. The group which deals with your exams will depend on where you are living at the time.

You can obtain syllabuses and exam regulations by writing to one of the examining boards in the relevant group and asking for an order form and price list.

● **London and East Anglian Group** (LEAG)

East Anglian Examinations Board, The Lindens, Lexden Road, Colchester CO3 3RL. Tel: (0206) 549595.
University of London School Examinations Board, Stewart House, 32 Russell Square, London WC1B 5DP. Tel: (01) 636 8000.

● **Midland Examining Group** (MEG)

University of Cambridge Local Examinations Syndicate, Syndicate Buildings, 1 Hills Road, Cambridge CB1 2EU. Tel: (0223) 61111.

● **Northern Examining Association** (NEA)

Joint Matriculation Board, Manchester M15 6EU. Tel: (061) 273 2565.

Northern Regional Examinations Board, Wheatfield Road, Westerhope, Newcastle upon Tyne NE5 5JZ. Tel: (091) 286 2711.

Yorkshire and Humberside Regional Examinations Board, Scarsdale House, 136 Derbyshire Lane, Sheffield S8 8SE. Tel: (0742) 557 436.

● **Northern Ireland Schools Examinations Council** (NISEC)

Northern Ireland Schools Examinations Council, Beechill House, 42 Beechill Road, Belfast BT8 4RS. Tel: (0232) 704666.

● **Southern Examining Group** (SEG)

Associated Examining Board, Stag Hill House, Guildford, Surrey

GU2 5XJ. Tel: (0483) 506506.

● **Welsh Joint Education Committee** (WJEC)

Welsh Joint Education Committee, 245 Western Avenue, Cardiff CF5 2YX. Tel: (0222) 561231.

A/S Level

The **Advanced Supplementary** (A/S) level examination is a new examination which has just been introduced in Britain. Two A/S levels are equivalent to one A level qualification. A/S levels are ideal if you feel that it is too early to specialise, or wish to take a wider variety of subjects.

A Level

Many students come to Britain to take an **Advanced** (A) level course. Obtaining good passes at A level is one way of fulfilling the entry requirements for most degree courses at British universities and for some of the courses offered by other colleges of higher education (see table on page 25).

● Most subjects at A level are tested by **written examinations** at the end of the course, usually in June and July.

● Most A level courses last for **two years** although several schools and colleges offer intensive one-year A level courses.

● If you are successful in your A level examinations, you will be awarded a **grade** from A-E, in each subject.

● Most schools and colleges will require you to have obtained a **pass at GCSE** level, or equivalent (see section on overseas qualifications on page 18) in relevant subjects before allowing you to begin an A level course.

● A level examinations are prepared and marked by nine different examining boards located throughout Britain. Copies of **syllabuses and regulations** can be obtained by writing to the relevant board:

Associated Examining Board, Stag Hill House, Guildford, Surrey GU2 5XJ. Tel: (0483) 506506.*

Cambridge University Local Examinations Syndicate, 1 Hills Road, Cambridge CB1 2EU. Tel: (0223) 61111.*

University of London School Examinations Board, Publications Department, 50 Gordon Square, London WC1 0PJ.*

Joint Matriculation Board, Regulations and Syllabuses, Messrs J. Sherratt and Sons, Publishers, 78 Park Road, Timperley, Altrincham, Cheshire, WA14 5QQ.

Oxford and Cambridge Schools Examination Board, Elsfield Way, Oxford OX2 8EP. Tel: (0865) 54421. Also at 10 Trumpington Street, Cambridge CB2 1QB. Tel: (0223) 64326.

Oxford Delegacy of Local Examinations, Ewart Place, Summertown, Oxford OX2 7BZ. Tel: (0865) 542912.*

Southern Universities Joint Board for School Examinations, Cotham Road, Bristol BS6 6DD. Tel: (0272) 736042.

Welsh Joint Education Committee, 245 Western Avenue, Cardiff CF5 2YX. Tel: (0222) 561231.

Northern Ireland Schools Examinations Council, Beechill House, 42 Beechill Road, Belfast BT8 4RS. Tel: (0232) 704666.

The four examining bodies marked with a * hold **examinations overseas**. This enables students from overseas to obtain some of the required qualifications before coming to Britain to study.

For further information about taking examinations in your own country, write to the examining board or contact your local British Council office (see Appendix 1).

Scottish Certificate of Education (SCE)
If you go to a school in Scotland you may take slightly different types of examinations. SCE **standard grade** is more or less equivalent to the GCSE, and SCE **higher grade** is the Scottish equivalent of A level. Good results in SCE higher will enable you to enter a Scottish university, although A levels are also accepted.

You can obtain information about the Scottish examination system from the Scottish Examination Board, Ironmills Road, Dalkeith, Midlothian EH22 1LE. Tel: (031) 663 6601.

International Baccalaureate (IB)
Some students come to Britain to study for the **International Baccalaureate** as an alternative to A levels. It is a two year course and covers a wider range of subjects than the traditional A level course. On an IB course you have to take six subjects altogether; one subject must be your own native language and one must be a second language.

The IB qualification is widely accepted by universities, polytechnics and colleges of higher education in Britain. It is also accepted by universities in many other countries throughout the world.

For further information about the IB, and for a list of schools and colleges in Britain which offer courses leading to the IB, contact the International Baccalaureate Office, University of London Institute of Education, 18 Woburn Square, London WC1H 0NS. Tel: (01) 637 1682.

Vocational and professional qualifications

Vocational and professional courses are intended to train and qualify you for a particular **career**. Many of these courses are more practical than theoretical, and some people prefer this type of course.

Vocational courses

There are hundreds of different types and levels of vocational courses, in subjects ranging from secretarial studies to timber technology, from physiotherapy to furniture manufacture.

There are also many **external examining boards** which provide qualifications in vocational subjects. Different colleges offer exams set by different examining boards.

Listed below are five of the main examining bodies offering courses across more than 200 vocational subjects and providing internationally recognised qualifications.

- **Business and Technician Education Council** (BTEC), Central House, Upper Woburn Place, London WC1H 0HH. Tel: (01) 388 3288. Main areas covered: agriculture, business, catering, computing, construction, design, engineering, finance, science.

- **City and Guilds of London Institute**, 76 Portland Place, London, W1N 4AA. Tel: (01) 580 3050. Examples of some of the hundreds of subjects covered: agriculture, forestry, mining, chemical industries, engineering, business, computing, food and drink, textiles, clothing and footwear, printing and publishing, hotels and catering, vehicles.

- **London Chamber of Commerce and Industry** (LCCI), Marlowe House, Station Road, Sidcup, Kent DA15 7BJ. Tel: (01) 302 0261. Offers qualifications in four main areas: secretarial, secretarial languages, languages for industry and commerce, business studies.

- **Pitman Examination Institute**, Godalming, Surrey GU7 1UU. Tel: (0486) 85311. Mainly offers qualifications in business and commerce.

● **Royal Society of Arts** (RSA), 8 John Adam Street, Adelphi, London WC2N 6EU. Tel: (01) 930 5115. Qualifications in: business studies, language, English as a foreign language, teaching, secretarial studies.

Write to these examining boards for syllabuses and for general information about the qualifications — but write directly to the colleges for details of their courses.

Professional courses
In many professions and trades, **professional institutions** exist to set and maintain standards in the profession and to encourage the exchange of information and ideas. Membership of a professional institution provides you with a status (and letters after your name) which will help your career.

In some cases you *must* have obtained membership of the relevant professional institution before you can practise in your chosen profession. For example, if you wish to call yourself a Certified Accountant, you must pass the examinations of the Chartered Association of Certified Accountants, which will enable you to use the letters ACCA after your name.

To become a member of a professional institution, you have to take their own **qualifying examinations**. Most colleges of further and higher education run courses which prepare you for these examinations. If you already have a relevant degree or a vocational qualification, you may be given **exemptions** from certain parts of the course. This means you may be able to miss out some parts of the course and some sections of the examinations. Before enrolling on a professional course, check whether the qualifications you already have will give you any exemptions.

There are many external examining bodies offering professional qualifications and hundreds of colleges which offer courses for these qualifications. Write to the relevant professional institution (see Appendix 4) for information. They will also be able to provide you with a list of colleges offering courses leading to their qualifications.

For further information about vocational and professional courses and qualifications, you will find the following publications useful (see reading list on page 35 for details about these books):

● In the state sector:
   A Compendium of Advanced Courses in Colleges of Further and Higher Education
   Directory of Further Education

Higher Education in the UK
The Polytechnic Courses Handbook
The Directory of Technical and Further Education
● In the independent sector:
Where to Study in the UK: A Guide to Professional Qualifications,
    Colleges and Courses
Directory of Independent Training and Tutorial Organisations

Diploma of Higher Education (DipHE)

DipHE courses are two years in length and are roughly equivalent to the first two years of a degree course. A DipHE is a complete qualification in itself but can be converted into a degree by a further two years of study. A DipHE course is often taken by people who do not yet want to commit themselves to a degree course but may want to do so in the future. The entry requirements for a DipHE course are usually the same as those for a degree.

For further information about DipHE courses, consult *CNAA Directory of First Degree and Diploma of Higher Education Courses* (see reading list on page 35).

Polytechnic and college certificates and diplomas

Some polytechnics and colleges may offer courses leading to their own, internal qualifications but which are not validated by a recognised external examining body — sometimes because a suitable one does not exist.

If you are planning to take this type of course, make sure that:

● the qualifications you will obtain will be accepted by employers in your country;
● the course is accepted by your government for foreign exchange purposes;
● the course is acceptable to the Home Office.

Degrees

Universities, polytechnics and many colleges of higher education offer courses leading to degrees at undergraduate level (eg BA, BSc, BEng, BEd, LLB) and postgraduate level (eg MA, MBA, MSc, MPhil, PhD).

If an institution is offering British degrees, you must make sure that it has been **authorised** to do so by either:

● a Royal Charter (universities);
● the Council for National Academic Awards, CNAA (polytechnics

and colleges of higher education).

The Department of Education and Science (see Appendix 3) can supply a list of institutions which are authorised to offer degrees.

University degrees at undergraduate level
There are over 5,000 different degree subjects and combinations of subjects offered at universities throughout Britain.

● First degree courses are usually three years long.

● Sandwich courses — courses which include a period of work experience outside college — and degree courses at Scottish universities usually take four years.

● Courses leading to degrees in medicine, dentistry and architecture can take from three to seven years.

● Some universities offer four year courses especially for students from overseas. The four years are made up of one preparatory year plus three years of degree course. The preparatory year is for students whose school leaving certificate is not specialised enough to meet the normal university entrance requirements.

Sandwich courses are becoming more common in many colleges in England.

The **minimum entrance requirements** for a degree course are two A level passes (two A/S levels count as one A level) and three passes at GCSE. As there is a lot of competition for places at university, especially on very popular courses, students are often asked for *three* good A level results.

Most universities will accept equivalent overseas qualifications. Sometimes other qualifications, such as BTEC national diplomas, are also accepted.

The system of secondary education in Britain is changing rapidly at the moment and alternative types of qualifications are emerging. Different universities have different policies on what qualifications they will accept. Therefore, always check with the university itself to see if your qualifications are acceptable for the course you wish to take.

Methods of examination for degrees depend on the course. One common method is a written examination at the end of the second and third years plus a thesis or project. In some cases this is combined with **continous assessment.**

Degrees are awarded at **ordinary** level or at **honours** level. Honours degrees are graded into first class (highest level), upper second class (2.i), lower second class (2.ii) and third class.

Polytechnic and college of higher education degrees at undergraduate level

The Council for National Academic Awards (CNAA) validates all degrees provided by polytechnics and colleges of higher education. *No college or polytechnic can offer a degree without approval by the CNAA.*

Degree courses at polytechnics and colleges of higher education are often more practical or creative than those offered by universities. You are also more likely to be examined by project work and by continuous assessment. Polytechnics and colleges of higher education also tend to offer more sandwich courses than universities. CNAA degrees are of the same academic standard as university degrees and should be regarded as equivalent.

Some students prefer these more vocational courses and welcome the valuable work experience that you can gain. Many polytechnics (and some colleges) have strong connections with British companies and local industry. The knowledge and experience you can gain will help you when you start your career and perhaps meet employers looking for more than just qualifications.

Entry requirements are more or less the same as those for a

university degree course.

The books listed below are essential reference books for anyone trying to choose a degree course at a university, polytechnic or college of higher education. See the book list on page 35 for further details about these books.

Higher Education in the United Kingdom

Handbook of Degree and Advanced Courses in Institutes/Colleges of Higher Education, Colleges of Education, Polytechnics, University Departments of Education

Degree Course Guides

Polytechnic Courses Handbook

British Qualifications

How to Choose Your Degree Course

The Compendium of University Entrance Requirements

The Scottish Universities Council on Entrance, Entrance Guide

Postgraduate qualifications

Postgraduate courses are ones you can take after you have already obtained a degree (although in some cases a professional qualification will be accepted as an alternative to a degree).

Postgraduate courses can lead to:

- Diplomas and Certificates (one year);
- Masters degrees (one or two years);
- Research degrees — MPhil (one or two years), PhD (two or three years).

Study for a postgraduate qualification can involve either attendance at lectures and seminars, followed by final written exams, or a period of independent research and submission of a project or thesis. You may even find a course which is a combination of all these. The main reference book, which provides details of postgraduate courses and the entrance requirements is *Graduate Studies*. A book called *Higher Education in the United Kingdom* also gives information about postgraduate courses and qualifications (see book list on page 35).

American degrees

Some British institutions offer courses leading to American qualifications, with the option of taking part of the course in America. The best place to obtain information about American qualifications is the **Fulbright Commission** (UK/US Education Commission), 6 Porter Street, London W1M 2HR. Tel: (01) 486 7697.

FINAL POINTS

You are likely to find different institutions offering the same, or similar, courses but organising the courses in very different ways — for example, with different entrance requirements, a different qualification at the end of the course, or for different periods of time. You can only get complete information about a particular course from the institution offering that course. Before applying for any course at any institution, make sure you are clear about the following:

● What are the entrance requirements for this course?
● Will the qualifications I already have be accepted?
● What qualifications will I obtain at the end of the course?
● Is this qualification recognised and accepted by employers in my home country, or by the type of institution where I may wish to continue my studies?
● How long will the course take to complete?

Can I use the qualifications I have already obtained in my own country?

Entrance requirements for courses in Britain are usually stated in terms of British qualifications, but you may have gained some qualifications in your home country which are regarded as equivalent to British qualifications. Many students find, for example, that their own school leaving certificate is comparable to British GCSE level.

You can check whether your qualifications are comparable to British qualifications by contacting your local **British Council** office. Remember, however, that each institution can decide for itself which, if any, overseas qualifications it will accept — so check this with the institution before you apply.

CHOOSING A COLLEGE

Once you have decided on your course, the next step is to choose the type of **institution** which will suit your needs.

In Britain, there is an incredible variety of **institutions** — schools, colleges, universities, polytechnics and so on — which often offer the same or similar courses. Before you choose a school or college, you must decide which type of institution is going to be most suitable for you.

State sector primary and secondary schools

State sector schools, offering primary and secondary education, are normally not an option for children who are in Britain for a temporary period only, or who are coming to Britain specifically for the purposes of education. However, children (aged 5 to 16) whose parents are here on business or whose parents are studying at a British institution, can attend a local state school if they are going to be in Britain for more than six months.

Independent preparatory schools, secondary schools and public schools

- Ages 2–7   general pre-school education;
- Ages 7–11/13   general subjects and preparation for the Common Entrance Examination (which is an entrance requirement for many independent secondary or public schools);
- Ages 11–18   courses leading to GCSE and A levels.

There are over 2,000 independent schools in Britain. The choice is wide, but you can begin to narrow it down by asking yourself the following questions:

- Would I prefer a large school or a small school (schools can vary in size from under 100 pupils to over 1,000)?
- Would I prefer an all girls/all boys school, or a coeducational school?
- Would I prefer a boarding school, or a day school?

All independent schools must be **registered** with the government. There are also two organisations which inspect and approve independent preparatory, secondary and public schools:

— **The Independent Schools Joint Council** (for schools in England)
— **The Scottish Council of Independent Schools** (for schools in Scotland).

     Information about independent schools in Britain can be obtained from the following sources:

— **Gabbitas, Truman and Thring,** 6–8 Sackville Street, Piccadilly, London W1X 2BR. Tel: (01) 734 0161. They provide a free advisory service to help you to choose a school; they will obtain prospectuses for you and put you in contact with the schools of your choice.
— **Independent Schools Information Service,** 56 Buckingham Gate, London SW1E 6AG. Tel: (01) 630 8790. This service offers information and advice on recognised independent schools in Britain. They also provide a **placement service** which is run from

offices in several countries overseas. Contact the London office for information about this service.

How to apply

Unfortunately, places at some of the more popular schools, and especially at boarding schools, are filled several years in advance. If possible, apply at least one year before you want to go to the school. Apply in writing, directly to the Head of the school.

The following sample letter shows the sort of information which you should include in your letter of application:

Dear Sir,

I would like to apply for a place at your school for my son, Timothy Chang. He is twelve years old and was born in Hong Kong on October 31st 1976. If possible, I would like him to start school in the September term of next year, 1989.

He is at present a pupil in the fifth grade at Hang Seng school in Kowloon, Hong Kong. We have been very pleased with his academic progress so far; he has passed all his end of year examinations with high grades, averaging around 70%. His best subject seems to be Mathematics.

He has been learning English since he was six years old, and we feel that his English is very good. I am enclosing a report from his present Headmaster but if you require any further information please contact me.

I look forward to hearing from you soon.

Yours faithfully,

Entrance requirements

Entrance requirements depend on the school, but most will require at least one and often a combination of the following:

● test or exam
● interview

- previous school report
- satisfactory results in previous exams.

Guardians

Many schools in Britain require that children under the age of sixteen should have someone to act as their **guardian**, if they are not being accompanied by one or both parents. The guardian will be responsible for the child during the term-time and in the school holidays if he or she cannot return home. The guardian should also be someone whom the school can contact in case of an emergency. The guardian can be a friend or relative who is already living in England.

If you cannot find a suitable person yourself, then **Gabbitas, Truman and Thring** (see page 19) provide a guardian service and will find suitable people to act as guardians on your behalf.

Independent colleges of further and higher education

These offer courses leading to:

- GCSE
- A levels
- International Baccalaureate
- Professional and vocational qualifications
- English language qualifications
- Degrees

Because independent colleges offering courses for students above the age of 16 are independent of government control, their quality and efficiency is not monitored by the government.

However, in Britain there are several organisations which **accredit**, (inspect, approve and monitor) the standards of independent colleges. The **accreditation** schemes which cover the widest range of colleges are run by:

— **The British Accreditation Council for Independent Further and Higher Education (BACIFHE),** Whitehart Lane, Tottenham N17 8HR. Tel: (01) 368 1299.

— **The Conference for Independent Further Education (CIFE),** c/o Colonel J Parkes (Secretary), Lovehayne Farm, Southleigh, Colyton, Devon EX13 6JE. Tel: (0404) 87241.

BACIFHE and CIFE accredit only those colleges which meet certain standards in teaching, student welfare, control and supervision of students, school premises and facilities and administration. Write to

BACIFHE and CIFE for a list of accredited colleges, or to your local British Council Office.

Several other organisations accredit schools and colleges offering courses in certain specialist areas of study. The main ones are:

— **The Association for the Recognition of Business Schools (ARBS)**, 8 Green Lane, Fordingbridge, Hampshire SP6 1HT. This accredits colleges which offer courses in business and management studies.
— **The Independent Secretarial Teaching Association**, 16 Marlborough Crescent, London W4 1HF. This accredits colleges offering training in secretarial studies.
— **Information Technology Training Accreditation Council (ITTAC)**, c/o BCM, London WC1N 3XX. This accredits training in information technology.

Accreditation is not compulsory; many well established independent colleges which offer high quality teaching have chosen not to apply for accreditation. Don't assume that any college which is not accredited is not a good college. However, you may feel safer if you apply to an accredited college, especially if you are coming from overseas and don't have a chance to look at the college yourself.

You can obtain lists of independent colleges in Britain and further information about other accreditation schemes from the following books (see reading list on page 35 for further details):
The Directory of Independent Training and Tutorial Organisations
The Gabbitas, Truman and Thring Guide to Independent Further Education

State sector colleges of further education and colleges of technology
For courses leading to:

● GCSE
● A levels
● BTEC and other vocational qualifications
● Professional qualifications
● English language qualifications
● Degrees

There are over 800 state sector colleges of further education in Britain of different sizes and offering different courses. This category also includes a wide range of specialist colleges; for example, colleges of art, colleges of agriculture, or colleges of printing.

British students aged 16 or 17 sometimes choose to take their A levels at a college of further education as an alternative to staying on in the sixth form of their school. The colleges are often less formal than schools, and offer a wider range of teaching methods. They also often offer a wider range of subjects to choose from.

Most students, however, go to colleges of further education to take vocational and professional courses. Some colleges also have links with nearby polytechnics and universities and run courses which lead directly onto a degree course at the polytechnic or university.

The best source of information on colleges of further education and the courses which they offer is *The Directory of Further Education* (see page 35 for details).

State colleges of higher education
For courses leading to:

- Degrees
- Postgraduate qualifications
- Professional qualifications
- Vocational qualifications
- Diplomas of Higher Education

There are nearly 200 state colleges of higher education in Britain. This category also includes colleges of education, colleges of art and design, schools and academies of music and drama. The term 'higher education' also covers universities, polytechnics and central institutions but these will be dealt with separately in the following two sections.

The main differences between colleges of higher education and universities and polytechnics is that the colleges are usually:

- smaller, and therefore more personal;
- more flexible in the combinations of subjects allowed;
- more flexible in allowing students to transfer from one course to another;
- less conventional in the choice of subjects at degree level, for example dance, drama, film.

These books offer information on colleges of higher education and the courses they run:

Colleges and Institutions of Higher Education Guide
Handbook of Degree and Advanced Courses in Institutes/Colleges of Higher Education, Colleges of Education, Polytechnics and University Departments of Education
A Compendium of Advanced Courses in Colleges of Further and

Higher Education
Higher Education in the United Kingdom
The Student Book
(See reading list on page 35 for further details)

Polytechnics and central institutions
For courses leading to:

- Degrees
- Postgraduate qualifications
- Vocational qualifications
- Professional qualifications
- Diplomas of Higher Education

There are 31 polytechnics in England and Wales and 16 central institutions, their equivalent, in Scotland. As well as the traditional range of courses, many polytechnics are now offering **modular courses and transferable credit schemes**. A student on this type of course can build up a degree by accumulating credits in a range of related subjects. Students can also gain credits towards a degree in their home country.

For information about polytechnics and central institutions, and the courses they offer, use the following books:

The Student Book
Polytechnic Courses Handbook
Directory of First Degree and Diploma of Higher Education Courses
Scottish Central Institution Handbook
(See reading list on page 35 for details).

Universities
For courses leading to:
- Degrees
- Postgraduate qualifications
- Professional qualifications

There are 62 universities and university colleges in Britain, ranging from very old and traditional to very modern, but each having its own individual character. There is also one independent university in England, the University of Buckingham. Universities are traditionally concerned with academic quality and are centres of research and knowledge. However, many now offer more practical and vocational courses as well.

The other main differences between universities and other types of institutions of higher education is the way courses are presented and taught. Universities often direct students towards knowledge instead of simply giving them facts, and expect more private study from their students.

As part of the course, you will normally have to write a **dissertation**, which is a type of project or a report of your own research. This will count towards your final assessment.

You can obtain further information about universities and the courses they offer from the following books (see reading list on page 35):

The Student Book
Choosing Your Degree Course
Degree Course Guide

SUMMARY — INSTITUTIONS AND THE COURSES THEY OFFER

Courses	*Institution*
GCSE	Independent school Independent college of further and higher education State college of further education
A level	Independent school Independent college of further and higher education State college of further education
International Baccalaureate	Independent school Independent college of further and higher education State college of further education
Courses leading to a vocational qualification	Independent college of further and higher education State college of further education State college of higher education Polytechnic and central institution
Courses leading to a professional qualification	State college of further education State college of higher education Independent college of further and higher education

	Polytechnic and central institution
	University
Diploma of Higher Education	State college of higher education
	Polytechnic and central institution
CNAA degree course	State college of higher education
	Polytechnic and central institution
	State college of further education (few)
University degree course	University
Postgraduate course	Polytechnic and central institution
	State college of higher education
	University

With so many institutions and courses available, it is not easy to choose the right place for your further education, so be thorough when you look for information.

The word **college** will be used to describe all types of further and higher education institute (universities, polytechnics, colleges of further and higher education, and so on) for the rest of this book.

The first steps in choosing

With such a wide variety of colleges offering the same, or a very similar, range of courses, how do you make your decision?

1. Choose your course — that is, the subject(s) and the level at which you wish to study.
2. Use the guides and directories referred to in the reading list on page 35 to make a list of all the colleges which offer the course you want.
3. Send for the prospectus.

Prospectuses

A **prospectus** is a booklet, produced by the college, which provides information about the college, the courses and how to apply.

Never apply to a school, college, polytechnic or university if you have not seen a copy of its prospectus.

If you write to a college, they should send you a free copy. Most British Council offices overseas will also have some prospectuses.

A good prospectus will provide answers to most of the questions you will want to ask about a college. If you cannot find the information you require in the prospectus, write to the college, or even telephone, to get the information. The more details a prospectus provides, the better. Beware of prospectuses which are vague and evasive, or of colleges which seem to avoid your questions.

Prospectuses are often written for British students, although some colleges produce additional booklets especially written for students from overseas.

Of course, the best way to find out about a college is to talk to someone who has studied there. If you have any friends who are in Britain, ask them to go and look at the college for you.

Making your choice

There are many things you have to consider before making a final decision about a college. The following list shows you the kinds of things to think about when you are making your choice.

Location
- Would you prefer to live and study in a large city or a small town?
- Would you prefer a **campus** or a **non-campus** college? A campus college is one where all the facilities, including the accommodation, classrooms, library, social areas, shops, sports facilities and so on, are all together on one site, sometimes just outside the main town. In a non-campus institution, the departments and facilities may be spread around the town or city.

Size and student numbers
- Would you prefer a large college where you will find students studying a wide variety of different types of courses, or a smaller one which might have a stronger sense of community?
- Will most of the other students be British or will there be a lot of other students from overseas? Which would you prefer?

Dates and length of courses
- Are the dates of the terms stated in the prospectus?
- Are these dates convenient for you? Will you be able to get to Britain on time?
- How long does the *whole* course last?
- Can you afford the time?

Fees
- Is the cost of the course clearly stated in the prospectus?
- Is it clear what is covered by the fees, and what the fees do *not*

include?

● Can you afford the fees for the *whole* course, or series of courses you need to take? Don't forget that the course or courses may last for several years and that the fees are likely to increase every year.

● Are there any regulations concerning how the fees must be paid? Do you have to pay the fees for a whole year at the beginning of the course, or can you pay termly, every few months?

The course

● What qualifications will you gain at the end of the course?

● Have you seen an outline of the content of the course? Will you be taught all the topics you need for the exams you want to take? This is especially important if the college is offering a course leading to an exam set by an external examining board.

● What can you do if you are not satisfied with the course? Can you transfer to another course?

Teaching methods

● How many students will be taught in one group?

● Which methods are used? Is the emphasis on large groups (lectures), small discussion groups (seminars or tutorials), private study or a combination of different approaches? Which suits you best?

Examination methods

● Will you have to take exams at the end of each year?

● Is there any continuous assessment?

● Will you be required to do a project or write a dissertation?

● Which form of assessment suits you best?

Entrance requirements

● Have you got the necessary entrance requirements for the course?

● Does the college accept overseas qualifications?

What happens if you fail?

● Are the procedures clear if you fail any part of the course?

● Can you re-take exams? If so, how long do you have to wait before you can?

● Will you have to re-take exams? If so, how long do you have to wait before you can?

● Will you have to re-take the whole course or any part of the course before you can re-take exams? These are important considerations for financial reasons.

Qualifications you will gain
- Is the qualification you will receive an **internal** one (exams set and marked by the college), or an **external** one (public exams set and marked by an external examining board)?
- Is the qualification you will receive accepted by employers in your country or by the type of college where you might want to continue your studies?

Facilities
- Does the college have its own library?
- Are there sports facilities in or near to the college?
- Is there a restaurant, café or bar?
- Is there a students' common room?
- Does the college organise social activities or outings?
- Is there a student welfare service?
- Does the college provide accommodation, or help you to find accommodation?
- Will the college provide advice for the next stage of your studies, or career advice?
- Is there a society for overseas students?
- Does the college have all the facilities you would like it to have?

Students with disabilities
It is a general policy of colleges and universities, *not* to discriminate against applicants on the grounds of disability. This means that your application for a place on a course should be accepted or rejected purely on the basis of your academic ability, along with all other applicants, and the fact that you may be disabled should not make any difference. However, not all colleges provide good facilities for disabled students.

Many of the older style buildings were certainly not designed for disabled people and are often inaccessible for people with visual disabilities or people in wheelchairs. Most colleges built recently have been more thoughtfully designed. Some colleges, *but not all*, also provide or organise:

- trained and qualified staff to advise and support students with disabilities;
- special equipment and facilities, including text books and computer keyboards in braille, wheelchair lifts;
- committees for disabled students, providing the opportunity to share views and make recommendations for improved facilities.

The college prospectus should tell you what the college does for disabled students. For further information and advice, contact **Skill: National Bureau for Students with Disabilities,** 336 Brixton Road, London SW9 7AA. Tel: (01) 274 0565.

How to apply
In further and higher education, different colleges and different courses require different methods of application. Methods of application can be divided into two main types; applications made **directly to the college** and applications made **through a central system** which deals with applications for colleges.

Applications made directly to the college
- Find details of when and how to apply from the prospectus.
- Use the college application form which should have been sent with the prospectus.
- You can apply to as many different colleges as you like.
- Don't leave it too late to make your application. Many colleges start processing applications and filling places about one year before the course is due to begin.

Applications made through central systems
Each central system has its own special **application form.** Before you complete an application to a central system, always read the **guidelines** which will be sent to you with the form. These guidelines will explain how to complete and return the form and when the closing date for applications is.

1. Write to the appropriate central system and obtain an application form.
2. Read the booklet which you will be sent, which tells you how to complete the form.
3. Complete the form and attach your entrance fee.
4. Pass on the form and your fee to your **referee**. This is the person who will write a reference for you, usually the head of your present or previous school.
5. Your referee (*not you*) must then return the form directly to the central system.

Central Register and Clearing House — CRCH

- Through CRCH you can apply for three different courses/colleges at one time.
- The fee for applying through CRCH is currently £6.

HOW DO I APPLY?

Course	Method of Application	Name of Central System	When to Apply
All courses at independent colleges	Direct to college	—	Any time. The sooner, the better.
All BEd courses (except at universities), some CNAA degree courses, and all DipHE courses at state colleges of higher education)		CRCH	From 15th September to 15th December
All courses at colleges of education in Scotland	Central system	Advisory Service on Entry to Teaching, 5 Royal Terrace, Edinburgh EH7 5AF	
All courses at colleges of education in N Ireland	Central system	Dept. for Education for Northern Ireland, Rathgael House, Balloo Road, Bangor, Co. Down	
All art and design courses at CNAA degree level and at BTEC level at state colleges of further and higher education in England and Wales		ADAR	From February to mid-March
All other courses at state colleges of further and higher education	Direct to college		About one year before start of course
Non-degree courses at polytechnics and all courses at central institutions	Direct to college		About one year before start of course
CNAA first degrees at polytechnics and some colleges of higher education	Central system	PCAS	From 1st September to 15th December
First degree courses at universities	Central system	UCCA	From 1st September to 15th December
First degree course at University of Buckingham	Direct to college		As soon as possible
First degree courses at Oxford or Cambridge	Direct to college and central system	UCCA	From 1st September to 15th October
Postgraduate courses at colleges of higher education, polytechnics and universities	Direct to college		About one year before start of course
Postgraduate teaching course (PGCE)	Central system	GTTR	From 15th September to 15th December

- You can obtain an application form from CRCH, 3 Crawford Place, London W1H 2BN (send a self-addressed envelope and and international reply coupon for the cost of postage).
- If you are a student from a commonwealth country (*except* Australia, Canada, New Zealand, Sri Lanka), *don't* apply through CRCH but through the education authority in your country.

Art and Design Admissions Registry — ADAR

- Through ADAR you can apply for two different courses/colleges at one time.
- The fee for applying through ADAR is currently £5.
- You can obtain an application form from ADAR, Penn House, 9 Broad Street, Hereford HR4 9AP. Tel: (0432) 266653.
- Applications for degree courses and for BTEC courses have to be made using separate application forms.

Graduate Teacher Training Registry — GTTR

- For applications for postgraduate teacher training (PGCE) courses.
- You can obtain an application form from GTTR, Crawford Place, London W1H 2BN (send a large self-addressed envelope and an international reply coupon).

Polytechnics Central Admissions System — PCAS

- Through PCAS you can apply for four different courses/colleges at one time.
- The fee charged is currently £6.
- Application forms and an explanatory booklet can be obtained from PCAS, PO Box 67, Cheltenham, Gloucestershire GL50 3AP. Tel: (0242) 526225.
- You can make your applications through PCAS from September 1st of *the year before* you wish to begin a course.
- Students from Cyprus, Guyana, India, Luxembourg, Mauritius, Tanzania and Thailand, should *not* apply through PCAS. These students should apply through their High Commission or Embassy in Britain (addresses listed below).

Universities Central Council on Admissions — UCCA

- Through UCCA you can apply for five different courses/colleges at one time.
- The fee charged is currently £6.
- You can obtain an application form and booklet from UCCA,

PO Box 28, Cheltenham, Gloucestershire GL50 1HY. Tel: (0242) 519091.
- Students from Cyprus, Guyana, India, Luxembourg, Mauritius, Tanzania and Thailand should *not* apply through UCCA. These students should apply through either the British Council or their High Commission or Embassy in Britain at the addresses listed below.
- Private students from Ghana should apply through the Scholarship Secretariat, PO Box M75, Accra.

Cyprus: The Cultural Counsellor, Cyprus High Commission, 93 Park Street, London W1Y 4ET.

Guyana: The Education Attaché, Guyana High Commission, 3 Palace Court, London W2 4LP.

India: The Counsellor (Science and Education), The High Commission of India, India House, Aldwych, London WC2B 4NA.

Mauritius   The Education Attaché, Mauritius High Commission, 32/33 Elvaston Place, London SW7.

Luxembourg: The Luxembourg Ambassador, Luxembourg Embassy, 27 Wilton Crescent, London SW1X 8SD.

Tanzania: The Educational Attaché, Tanzania High Commission, 43 Hereford Street, London W1Y 8DB.

Thailand: Thai Government Students Office, 28 Prince's Gate, London SW7 1QF.

Some DOs and DON'Ts when applying through UCCA
- UCCA asks you to list your five choices **in order of preference**. If you are applying for very popular courses, unfortunately you will probably be automatically rejected by the university which is your fifth, and sometimes even fourth, choice.
- You can **bracket** choices, which means placing two or more as an equal choice. If you bracket two or three, *write them down in alphabetical order*.
- Try not to bracket all five — this will be seen as a lack of commitment to any university.
- Don't apply for lots of very different or unrelated subjects. If you apply to study maths at one university, art at another and German history at a third, you will be seen as someone who doesn't really know what they want to do.

FILLING IN FORMS

Whether you are completing a form for a central clearing system or a form for an individual college, it will be your first, and maybe your only, chance to make an impression. The appearance of the form and what you write on it is, therefore, very important.

Some DOs and DON'Ts
- Write in **black ink**. The forms usually get photocopied and black is better.
- Print or use **block capitals**. Don't use joined writing.
- Don't start to write directly onto the form. Write your answers to the questions on **another piece of paper** first. When you are satisfied that there are no mistakes, copy what you have written onto the form.
- If you have to cross anything out, **do it with a ruler**.
- Check for **spelling mistakes**, or better still, get someone else to check it for you.
- Keep a **photocopy** of the form for yourself. By the time you are asked to go for an interview, you may have forgotten what you wrote.
- Make full use of the section which asks you to write about yourself. Don't just say things like, 'I like sport', or 'I like films'. Say **what** sport your like, **which** films you like, and **why**.
- Don't apply for a course at a college which does not offer that course. This may sound obvious but some people have done this. They obviously did not read the prospectus!
- If your native language uses a different script, you must decide how you want to spell your name in English. Always use the same spelling each time you write your name.
- In Britain the word 'surname' means your family name.

An offer of a place
The application process begins many months before you want to begin a course, but you will not be certain of a place on a course until much nearer the time. Many offers of places are **conditional** on your forthcoming exam results. This means that the college will reserve a place for you but you will only be able to accept it if you achieve the exam grades they ask for.

If you are lucky, or if you are not going to take any exams, you may be given an **unconditional** offer, one which does not depend on examination results.

If you have applied through UCCA and/or PCAS, and if more

than one college offers you a place on a course, you are permitted to accept **two offers** (two from UCCA and two from PCAS) until May 15th. After this date you will be asked to specify which of the two is your first choice.

If you have applied directly to a number of colleges, you can accept as many offers as you like, but don't forget to inform the colleges you are rejecting, when you have made your final choice.

If your applications are rejected
If you have applied through UCCA, PCAS or CRCH, there are two more steps you can take. Details of both will be sent to you automatically by the central system.

In February: Continuing Application Procedure (CAP). If you have not yet received any offers of a place, CAP gives you the opportunity to make fresh applications to other colleges.

In August: Clearing System. If you still have not received any offers, or if you have not obtained the required grades in your examinations, you may still be able to find a place through the clearing system.

Choosing a course and a college — details of books which you will find useful
Some of the books listed below are very expensive. As you may only need to use them once or perhaps twice in your life it is not a good idea to buy them all. You will find some of them in large libraries, and many of them at your local British Council office. Some schools and colleges may also have them in their libraries. The prices quoted were accurate in 1989.

- *A Compendium of Advanced Courses in Colleges of Further and Higher Education*, London and South-Eastern Advisory Council for Further Education, Tavistock House South, Tavistock Square, London WC1H 9LR. £3.60.
- *British Qualifications*, Kogan Page, 120 Pentonville Road, London N1 9JN. £17.50.
- *CNAA Directory of First Degree and Diploma of Higher Education Courses*. CNAA, 344-354 Gray's Inn Road, London WC1X 8BP. Free.
- *CNAA Directory of Post Graduate and Post Experience Courses*, CNAA (address as above). Free.
- *Colleges and Institutions of Higher Education Guide*, The Standing Conference of Principals and Directors of Colleges

and Institutes of Higher Education, Edge Hill College of HE, Ormskirk, Lancashire L39 4QP. Free.

- *Degree Course Guides*, CRAC, Hobson's Press, Bateman Street, Cambridge CB2 1LZ. £3.50 each (individual booklets covering subjects offered by universities).
- *Directory of Further Education*, CRAC, Hobson's Press, Bateman Street, Cambridge CB2 1LZ. £44.
- *Directory of Independent Training and Tutorial Organisations*, E Summerson and M Davies, Careers Consultants Ltd., 12–14 Hill Rise, Richmond, Surrey TW10 6UA. £12.95.
- *Directory of Technical and Further Education*, Consumer Services Department, Longman Group UK Ltd, 4th Avenue, Harlow, Essex CM19 5AA. £43.
- *Gabbitas, Truman and Thring Guide to Independent Further Education*, Gabbitas, Truman and Thring, 6, 7 & 8 Sackville Street, London W1X 2BR. £9.95.
- *Graduate Studies*, CRAC, Hobson's Press, Bateman Street, Cambridge CB2 1LZ. £69.75.
- *Handbook of Degree and Advanced Courses in Institutes/ Colleges of Higher Education, Colleges of Education, Polytechnics, University Departments of Education*, CRCH, Linneys ESL Ltd, Newgate Lane, Mansfield, Nottinghamshire. NG18 2PA. £9.
- *Higher Education in the United Kingdom*, Consumer Services Department, Longman Group Uk Ltd, 4th Avenue, Harlow, Essex CM19 5AA. £11.95.
- *How to Choose Your Degree Course*, Brian Heap, Careers Consultants Ltd, 12–14 Hill Rise, Richmond, Surrey TW10 6UA. £9.95.
- *Scottish Central Institution Handbook*, Paisley College of Technology, High Street, Paisley PA1 2BE, Scotland. Free.
- *University Entrance: The Official Guide*, Sheed and Ward, 2 Creechurch Lane, London EC3A 5AQ. £9.95.
- *The Polytechnic Courses Handbook*, Committee of Directors of Polytechnics, Kirkman House, 12–14 Whitfield Street, London W1P 6AX. £9.50.
- *The Scottish Universities Council on Entrance, Entrance Guide, SUCE*, Kinnessburn, Kennedy Gardens, St Andrews KY16 9DR, Scotland. £2.
- *The Student Book*, Klaus Boehm and Nick Wellings, Careers Consultants Ltd, 12–14 Hill Rise, Richmond, Surrey TW10 6UA. £8.95.

● *Where to Study in the UK: A Guide to Professional Qualifications, Colleges and Courses*, Kogan Page, 120 Pentonville Road, London N1 9JN. £5.95.

2
English Language, Schools and Courses

IS MY ENGLISH GOOD ENOUGH?

Before you decide to come to Britain to study, consider whether your English is good enough. There are many reasons for this:

● Most colleges will ask for a recognised qualification in English language as part of their normal entrance requirements.
● If your English is weak, you won't be able to make the most of your course or be successful in your examinations. You must be able to express your knowledge in clear, comprehensible English.
● If you cannot communicate with British people, you may become isolated and lonely.

In order to cope with your course and to get the most from your time in Britain, you must be able to **speak, write** and **understand** English well.

Some colleges test your English before they allow you to enrol on a course. Others ask for evidence that you have passed a recognised test before they accept you on a course. Different colleges and different courses will have different requirements. In general, the normal minimum English language requirement for entry onto a course of *higher education* is a pass in one of the following:

● English O level (pre-1988), or GCSE English;
● Joint Matriculation Board (JMB) Test in English for Overseas Students, grade three or above;
● Associated Examining Board Test in English for Educational Purposes, grade three or above.

Some institutions will also accept:

● TOEFL, score 550 or above;
● The Cambridge Proficiency Examination;
● The British Council ELTS test, grade six or above.

38

As there are so many different qualifications in English language, you must find out which one is accepted by the college where you have chosen to study.

If you want to check your standard of English before you come to Britain, you should contact your local British Council office and ask to take the **English Language Testing Service** (ELTS) test. This will tell you whether any further English language tuition is necessary for a particular course.

If you need to improve your English, there are many different ways of doing so:

● Attend classes in your own country, before coming to Britain. Make sure that the classes lead to the qualification you require.

● Attend classes at the college or university where you intend to study. Many institutions offer English courses which start **before** your main course begins. These courses can last from one month to twelve months.

● Attend a state sector or independent sector English language school. Again, make sure that the course you take will lead to a recognised qualification.

LEARNING ENGLISH IN BRITAIN

There are many reasons why you may want to come to Britain to study English language, and as many different types of courses for your needs.

● For pleasure, to learn to speak and understand another language **(English as a Foreign Language — EFL)**.

● To learn English because you intend to study at a British school, college or university **(English for Academic Purposes — EAP)**.

● To learn English for a specific purpose. For example, English for business, English for engineers, English for doctors, English for teachers **(English for Special Purposes — ESP)**

● To learn English because you intend to live in an English speaking country **(English as a Second Language — ESL)**.

You will also find:
— short courses (two or three weeks);
— long courses (six months to one year);
— courses which combine the study of English with a holiday in England;
— courses which combine the study of English with a hobby (for example horse riding, tennis, photography, computer

programming), or which combine the study of English with lessons in other subjects so that you can gain another qualification.

WHAT SORT OF ENGLISH LANGUAGE SCHOOL SHOULD YOU CHOOSE?

As with most other areas of education in Britain, you can choose between state schools and independent schools.

State sector English language schools

State sector colleges of further and higher education organise a wide range of academic courses which both British students and students from overseas can attend. Some of these colleges also provide classes in English language for students from overseas. Students who study English at a state sector college are able to socialise with British students, and to find out what life at a British college is really like.

You can obtain a list of state sector colleges offering English language courses, and details of the courses which are available, from **The British Association of State Colleges in English Language Teaching (BASCELT)**, c/o Hampstead Garden Suburb Institute, Central Square, London NW11 7BN.

Independent sector English language schools

The best guide to English language courses and schools in the independent sector comes from an organisation called **The Association of Recognised English Language Teaching Establishments (ARELS-FELCO)**, 125 High Holborn, London WC1V 6QD. Tel: (01) 242 3136. Write directly to them for their free handbook or ask for details at your local British Council office.

All schools listed in the ARELS–FELCO handbook have been inspected and recognised by the British Council, and are re-inspected every three years. In their inspection, the British Council check things like the standards of teaching, the classrooms, the student welfare service, and the administration of the school.

Another publication which you may find useful is: *The Gabbitas, Truman and Thring Guide to English Language Schools,* Gabbitas, Truman and Thring (address on page 19), £6.95.

Whether you choose a state sector school, an independent school which has been recognised by the British Council or one which has not been recognised, there are a number of points to consider and questions to ask yourself *before* you enrol on any course.

Questions to ask yourself
● Why am I taking an English course?

- Will the course I have chosen teach me the type of English I need?
- Is the course the right length for me — can I afford the time and the money?
- If I need a qualification in English, does this course lead to the right qualification?
- Is the qualification recognised in my home country?
- Is the qualification recognised by the school or college where I am going to continue my studies?
- Would I prefer to study English with students from my home country, or with students from other countries?
- Would I prefer to live in a hostel, or accommodation with an English family?
- How do I best learn a language — by classroom teaching, or by conversation with people, or by a mixture of both?

There are also things you need to find out about the school. If you can't find the answer to the following questions in the school's prospectus, then write to or telephone the school and ask for the information you require.

Questions to ask the school
- How many students are taught in one class?
- Will everyone in a class be from the same country or from different countries?
- How many hours of **classroom** tuition will be provided in a week?
- Are the teachers qualified and experienced?
- What do the fees include?
  - tuition only?
  - outings and activities?
  - accommodation?
  - books?
  - examination fees?
- Does the school organise social events and outings to places of interest?
- Does the school provide accommodation, or help students to find accommodation?
- Does the school have a coffee bar or restaurant, or somewhere for students to go to during breaks?
- Does the course lead to any examinations and qualifications?
- Are the examinations **internal** (set and marked by teachers in the

school) or **external** (set and marked by an external organisation)?
- If there are no exams to take, does the school provide a certificate of attendance at the end of the course?

What qualifications can I obtain?

If you wish to obtain a qualification in English language, there are many different ones to choose from. The most suitable examination for you will depend on your level of English, and the type of English language tuition you are receiving (EFL,EAP,ESP and so on).

Before enrolling on a course which leads to an examination, make sure that the course is the right level for you, and that the qualification is the one you need. The school should be able to help you to choose the right course and examination.

There are several external examining boards offering internationally recognised qualifications in the English language. The chart below lists the main examinations you can take in England and the examining boards which offer the qualification.

EXAMINATIONS IN ENGLAND

Exam Board	Type of Exam	Skills Tested	Comments
Associated Examining Board, Stag Hill House, Guildford, Surrey GU2 5XJ (0483) 506506	Test in English for Educational Purposes.	Reading Writing	EAP
ARELS Examining Board, 125 High Holborn, London WC1V 6QD (01) 242 3136	Preliminary Certificate Higher Certificate Diploma	All levels: speaking, and understanding spoken language	
Educational Testing Service, Princeton, NJ, USA	TOEFL exam	Listening comprehension, reading comprehension, written English	This exam is for students wishing to study at an American college, but is accepted by many colleges in Britain and abroad
English Speaking Board, 32 Norwood Avenue, Southport, Merseyside PR9 7EG (0704) 231366	Assessment in Spoken English	Speaking	
Institute of Linguists, Mangold House, 24a Highbury Grove, London N5 2EA (01) 359 7445	Certificate in EFL Diploma in EFL	Speaking, reading, listening, writing Speaking, writing, interpreting, translating	
Joint Matriculation Board, Manchetser M15 6EU (061) 273 2565	Test in English for Overseas Students	Writing, reading, understanding spoken English	EAP qualification accepted by colleges of HE
London Chamber of Commerce and Industry, Marlowe House, Station Rd, Sidcup, Kent DA15 7BJ (01) 302 0261	English for commerce (elementary) English for commerce (intermediate) English for commerce (advanced) Spoken English for commerce and industry (preliminary) Spoken English for commerce and industry (intermediate) Spoken English for commerce and industry (advanced)	Writing, reading Writing, reading speaking Writing, reading speaking Speaking, listening Speaking, listening Speaking, listening	English for commerce and/ or industry

EXAMINATIONS IN ENGLAND

Exam Board	Type of Exam	Skills Tested	Comments
Pitman Examination Institute, Cattleshall Manor Godalming, Surrey GU7 1UU (0486) 85311	EFL elementary EFL intermediate EFL advanced EFL communicative ESL	Reading, writing listening Reading, writing listening Reading, writing listening Readng, writing listening Reading, writing listening	

Royal Society of Arts, John Adam Street, Adelphi, London WC2N 6EZ (01) 930 5115	EFL – basic
	   – intermediate
	   – advanced
	Certificate and
	  Diploma for Overseas
	  Teachers of English
	EFL for Secretaries
	Spoken English
	  – Certificate
	  – Advanced Certificate
		Reading, writing	

Trinity College London, 11–13 Mandeville Place, London W1M 6AQ (01) 935 5773	Spoken English (12 grades) Intermediate English English for Overseas Teachers of English	Speaking, listening Writing	Specifically for students of ESL
University of Cambridge Local Examinations Syndicate, 1 Hills Road, Cambridge CB1 2EU (0223) 61111	Preliminary First Certificate Certificate of Proficiency in English Exams in English for language teachers	Reading, writing, speaking, listening Reading, writing, speaking, listening Reading, writing speaking, listening	
University of Oxford Delagacy of Local Examinations, Ewart Place, Summertown, Oxford OX2 7BZ (0865) 542912	Preliminary Certificate Higher Certificate	Reading, writing Reading, writing	EAP
General Medical Council, Overseas Registration Division, 153 Cleveland Street, London W1T 6DE (01) 387 2556	PLAB (Professional and Linguistic Assessment Board		Compulsory exam for doctors from overseas who wish to register in Britain
GCSE English A level English			See page 10

3
Money

Before you come to Britain to study and live, make sure that you can afford to.

- Can you afford the tuition fees for the *whole* course? Many courses last for more than one year. You may also need to take a series of courses before you gain the qualifications you need.
- Can you afford the living expenses for the *whole* time you will be in Britain?

TUITION FEES

At all *state sector* colleges, polytechnics and universities, there are two types of fees. There is a **home student (lower) rate** and the **overseas student (higher) rate**.

Who can pay the home rate of fees?

A few students from overseas are eligible to pay the home student rate of fees. In order to qualify for the home student rate you must satisfy the following conditions:

- You must have been **ordinarily resident** in Britain for at least three years before the beginning of your course (for a definition of ordinarily resident see page 61).
- For any part of that time, you must **not** have been **a full-time student**.

As with most regulations, there are some exceptions. Even if you do not meet the conditions described above, you may still be eligible to pay the home student rate of fees, if:

- you, your children or your wife/husband have been granted **refugee status** or 'Exceptional Leave to Remain' by the British government;

- you are part of a formal **student exchange** agreement;

- you have been granted **permanent residence** or **settled status** within the three years before the beginning of your course. (An example of this would be someone who had recently married a British citizen (see Chapter 4 for further details). If you are already on a course, however, getting married will *not* effect the rate of fee you pay.)

If you are from the EC, or are the child of someone from the EC, you may be able to have your fees paid for you by the British government. Check with your college for further details about this and how to apply. To be eligible you must:

- **have been resident** in the EC for three years prior to the start of the course;
- **not have previously attended** a course of advanced education;
- **not be receiving** a local authority grant.

Fee rates at state sector colleges — 1988/89

Overseas students

Universities	1st degree and postgraduate arts courses	1st degree and postgraduate Science courses	Clinical years (practical part of a degree in medicine or dentistry)
	£3,930	£5,180	£9,590
Polytechnics and other colleges of further and higher education	Advanced courses (degree level) £4,017	Non-advanced courses £2,225	

Home students

All 1st degree courses	All postgraduate courses	All non-advanced courses
£578	£1,800	£390

These are the recommended minimum fees. Some colleges will charge more.

The regulations regarding fee status are quite complicated. If you think that you should be paying fees at the home student rate, but your college is charging you the overseas rate, do the following:

1.   Ask the college to explain their reasons in writing.
2.   Contact either

     ● the welfare officer or student union officer at the college,
     ● a British Council office (see Appendix 1),
     ● UKCOSA (see Appendix 2).

     They will explain the regulations to you and advise you about what, if anything, you should do.
3.   **Do not pay any money** or sign any agreements to pay money if you think there has been a mistake about your fees. *You cannot change from an overseas fee rate to a home fee rate once you have started a course.*

Fees and costs depend on the course. Always obtain detailed and up-to-date information about fees directly from the college. This also applies to **independent sector colleges**; again, fees depend on the type and length of the course, so write to the college and ask for details.

The full cost of a course should be clearly shown in the college prospectus.

Some other points to consider

● Don't forget that the fees quoted for the first year of your course will probably increase the following year. Fees usually go up every year, even when you have already started your course.

● Before you begin a course, make sure that you will be able to afford the fees for the *whole* course.

● Many colleges now ask students from overseas for evidence that they can pay the fees and support themselves, *before* allowing the student to register.

● If you will need to take another course afterwards, find out how much that course will cost and make sure that you will be able to afford both courses.

● Make sure you know what the fees do and do not include. This should be made clear in the prospectus. If it is not clear, ask the college for the information you want.

When to pay

In many cases, tuition fees for the whole year must be paid in advance, when you **enrol** — that is, arrive at the college for the first day. Therefore, arrange for the money to be in Britain ready for your arrival.

Examples of things the fees might not include

Primary and secondary education	Further and higher education
uniform	examination fees
music lessons	text books
art equipment	science/art equipment
school outings	sports
textbooks	library fees
	science laboratory fees
	college activities
	Value Added Tax — 15%
	(an extra charge made by
	some schools and colleges)

Some colleges will allow you to pay each term, every three or four months, but some will not allow you to begin your course until you have paid the fees for the whole year.

● **Find out** if the college has regulations concerning fee paying *before* you leave your home country, then you can make the appropriate arrangements.

● **Try to avoid** paying any large sums of money (except deposits) to a college before you come to Britain yourself, just in case you fail to get entry clearance.

● If you are having money sent over to Britain in advance, **have it sent to a bank**, not directly to a college.

Deposits
Some colleges will require you to pay a **deposit** or a **registration fee**. That is, money paid in advance in order to secure you a place on a course.

If, for any reason, you find that you cannot come to Britain to study, you may lose your deposit. If a college does not refund deposits, it should say so in the prospectus or on the application form.

Many universities, polytechnics and state sector colleges of further and higher education now ask for something called **caution money** to be paid *when you arrive at the college*. This is refunded at the end of the course. This sum is currently £100, £50 for students from the EC.

Refunds

If you *do* have to pay any fees in advance, either before you come to Britain or after you have arrived, ask the college if some or all of the amount paid, can be **refunded** in certain circumstances. For example:

● if you are unable to come to Britain for any reason;
● if you have immigration problems, either entering the country or extending your permission to stay;
● if you are dissatisfied with the college;
● if you have to leave Britain unexpectedly.

Warning!

The majority of colleges in Britain are genuine and honest as far as money is concerned. However, there have been cases of colleges taking money from overseas students under false pretences. Fortunately, these are a small minority.

Two pieces of advice where fees are concerned:

1. Don't sign any agreements that you do not understand. Make sure you know *exactly* what you are agreeing to before you sign anything or hand over any money. If you don't understand what you are signing, get someone else to read it and explain it to you.

2. Before you pay any money, make sure you are clear about how much you will need to pay altogether, how you are going to pay it, when you have to pay it and exactly what you are paying for.

THE COST OF LIVING IN BRITAIN

Before coming to Britain, you should have some idea about how much money you will need for your living expenses while you are here. The amount you will need will depend on where in Britain you will be living and the type of accommodation you have.

In the year 1988/89, for example, the cost of living (excluding tuition fees) might be approximately:

A single student with no dependants   £4,000–5,500
living in London or the South East
of Britain

A single student living elsewhere in Britain	£3,500–4,000
A married couple	£6,000–8,000
Each child	£700–1,000

The cost of living in Britain usually increases by about 6% each year.

Many colleges will provide you with detailed information about the living costs in their area. You can also obtain information abut the cost of living in Britain from your local British Council office.

Train and coach fares from London

Destination	Train	Coach		Train	Coach		Train	Coach
Aberdeen	£59.00	£19.50	Bangor	£30.00	£16.50	Bath	£19.00	£8.60
Birmingham	£17.00	£9.20	Bradford	£32.00	£18.50	Brighton	£11.10	£5.80
Bristol	£19.00	£10.00	Cambridge	£9.10	£6.00	Cardiff	£25.00	£14.00
Chester	£24.00	£13.50	Coventry	£16.00	£7.40	Derby	£18.50	£9.20
Doncaster	£29.00	£13.50	Dover	£14.00	£7.80	Durham	£47.00	£14.00
Edinburgh	£50.00	£17.00	Exeter	£27.00	£14.00	Folkestone	£11.90	£7.40
Glasgow	£45.00	£19.00	Gloucester	£18.00	£10.00	Harrogate	£34.00	£19.50
Hull	£32.00	£16.00	Inverness	£59.00	£19.50	Lancaster	£30.00	£15.00
Leeds	£32.00	£17.50	Leicester	£14.50	£7.80	Liverpool	£26.00	£13.50
Manchester	£26.00	£13.50	Newcastle	£49.00	£14.00	Nottingham	£18.50	£9.60
Norwich	£17.50	£9.00	Oxford	£9.10	£6.00	Plymouth	£32.00	£17.50
Preston	£30.00	£13.00	Sheffield	£22.00	£13.50	Southampton	£11.90	£7.40
Swansea	£27.00	£16.50	York	£32.00	£16.00			

WHAT ARE PRICES LIKE IN BRITAIN?

The chart on page 50 is meant as a *rough guide only* to costs and prices of some of the things you will have to pay for while you are in Britain.

Travel within Britain — from London

The coach fares given are for **single**, or one-way, tickets. The train fares given are **Blue Saver Returns**. These tickets are available for journeys made on any day except Friday and after 9.30am. The tickets are **return** tickets, and last for one month. You will find that Blue Saver Returns are cheaper than ordinary single tickets, but before you buy your ticket, make sure that it is a Blue Saver day and time.

Accommodation

The main distinction is between living in accommodation provided by the college and private accommodation which you must find for yourself.

College accommodation for one academic year	In London	Outside London
For a single student including meals	£1,325	£1,070–£1,340
Excluding meals	£600–£900	£360–£750
For a couple/family	£2,000	£1,400
Private accommodation (per week)		
Bedsit	£25–£60	£18–£25
One bedroomed flat	£70–£90	£30–£50
Two bedroomed flat	£120–£150	£50–£80

Although private accommodation may seem to be far cheaper than college accommodation, don't forget that the price does not include things like heating, lighting, food and so on. Also living in non college accommodation will probably mean more travelling expenses. See Chapter 5 for more information on accommodation.

Gas and electricity

This only applies to students who are not living in college accommodation. Gas and electricity will be needed for heating, cooking and lighting. Of course, the amount you have to pay will depend on how much you use, but if you come from a hot country you will probably find that you are using a lot of heating, especially during the cold months (eight or nine months per year!).

For gas and electricity combined, averaged out over the whole year, you should expect to pay about:

- **£26 per month** for a room with an electric heater and a gas cooker;
- **£37 per month** for a small flat with gas heating and cooker;
- **£46 per month** for a small flat with electric heating and a gas cooker.

Clothing

The prices on page 53 provide a rough guide to good quality and reasonably fashionable clothes. If you are interested in particularly fashionable or **designer** clothes, then expect to pay more!

Washing clothes and dry cleaning

Very few students will have their own washing machines. It is likely that you will have to do your washing at a **launderette**, which is a place where washing machines are provided for the general public. Some colleges have their own launderettes.

Use of large washing machine	— £1.70
Use of small washing machine	— £1.20
Use of tumble drier	— £0.20
Washing powder	— £0.90–£1.20 for a medium sized packet

If you have some items which you can't wash (it will say so on the label) they will have to be **dry cleaned**. Drying cleaning is quite expensive. You should bear this in mind when you are buying clothes.

Suit	— £4–£5	Shirt/Blouse	— £1.50–£3
Trousers	— £2–£3	Skirt	— £1.50–£2.50
Jacket	— £2.50–£4	Coat	— £3–£5

Typical clothes prices

	men	*women*	*children*
Suit	£60–£80	£50–£60	
Warm overcoat	£40–£90	£40–£80	£12–£17
Light raincoat	£25–£40	£30	£12–£14
Casual jacket	£15–£40	£20–£35	£12–£16
Shoes	£15–£35	£12–£29	£5–£17
Boots	£20–£35	£20–£35	£12–£14
Shirt/blouse	£7–£20	£9–£25	£5–£10
Jumper/cardigan	£8–£20	£10–£25	£3–£11
Skirt	—	£13–£30	£5–£10
Trousers	£11–£25	£13–£30	£5–£10
Day dress	—	£14–£20	£6–£15
Smart dress	—	£20–£40	£10–£20
Jeans	£10–£29	£17–£29	£9–£15
Sweatshirt	£10–£17	£10–£17	£4–£12
T-shirt	£5–£12	£9–£13	£4–£6
Tracksuit	£17–£30	£15–£25	£7–£14
Running shoes	£10–£35	£12–£25	£5–£15
Nightwear	£9–£14	£10–£15	£15
Socks	£1–£3	£1–£3	70p–£2
Tights/stockings	—	99p–£5	—
Umbrella	£5–£10		
Children's pushchair	£50–£100		
Underwear			
Vest	£3–£6	—	99p–£3
Bra	—	£5–£10	—
Pants	£1.50–£5	£1–£3	75p–£3
Nappies (24)			£2.95–£3.95

Food

If you are living in college accommodation, you will not have to buy much food as most meals, and sometimes all meals, are provided for you. Make sure you eat as many meals there as you can, as you have already paid for them.

Some typical meals and their costs

		Cooked at home
(a)	Meal for one (meat, potatoes, one vegetable plus some fruit and cheese):	£1.50–£2
(b)	Cheap meal for one (omelette with salad and bread):	£1.10
(c)	Meal for two (same items as meal(a)):	£2.50–£3
(d)	Cheap meal for two (rice cooked with eggs plus two vegetable dishes, followed by fruit and yoghurt):	£2.20
(e)	Meal for four (chicken, rice, salad, bread, fruit, cheese):	£6–£7
And with the meal —	Bottle of wine Bottled water Fresh orange juice (per carton)	£1.99–£3.50 48p–75p £1

		In a cafe/ restaurant
(a)	Meal for one (fish and chips):	£1.20–£1.60
(b)	Meal for one (steak, chips, peas followed by apple pie):	£4–£7
(c)	Meal for two (chinese meal, three dishes plus rice):	£6–£8
(d)	Meal for two (pizza followed by ice-cream):	£10–£12
(e)	Meal for four (pasta, garlic bread, fruit, cheese):	£23.60
And with the meal —	Bottle of wine Bottled water Orange juice (per glass) Beer (per bottle)	£4.99–£7 £1–£2 30p–£1.30 £1.20

If you are going to eat in restaurants, you will find a great variety of prices. The restaurants at college are always cheaper than ones in the town.

If you are going to cook, you will find that cooking for several people, and sharing the cost of the meal, is always cheaper than cooking just for yourself. So if a group of you share the same kitchen, why not share meals too?

Other basic necessities

Soap	— 20p
Shampoo (medium sized bottle)	— 98p
Toothpaste (medium)	— 80p-£1
Toilet roll (2)	— 68p
Women's sanitary protection	— 75p-£1.50

Britain hasn't quite got used to metric measurements. Although you will find some products packaged in kilos, grams, metres or litres, you will also see many sold in the old non-metric pounds, ounces, pints, feet and inches. There is a conversion chart on page 191.

Social life

This depends on where you are living. Everything seems to be more expensive if you are living in a large city, especially London.

cinema	—	£2.80-£5
theatre	—	£2.50-£20 (depends where you sit)
disco	—	£2-£10
concert	—	£1.50-£15 (depends where, and what is on)
museum	—	many are free
sports	—	sports centres usually require you to become a member. Membership fees can be anything between £15 and £150.

Many places do have reduced rates for students, so always carry your **student card** with you. If your own college has facilities such as a cinema club, swimming pool, badminton courts, gymnasium, regular discos, music concerts, and so on, use them as much as possible. Facilities like these provided by the college are always much cheaper than those in the outside world. For example:

The cost of a typical night out in London

Tube fare to town	£1.20
Drinks for four	£5.00
A cinema ticket	£4.50
Your share of a meal	£6.00
Tube fare home	£1.20
	£17.90

Some guidelines on food prices

Milk (1 pint)	£0.25	Rice (1lb)	£0.50	Crisps (per packet)	£0.15
Bread	£0.45	Pasta (1lb)	£0.38	Chocolate (small)	£0.18
Butter	£0.56	Bacon (1lb)	£0.98	Beans (small tin)	£0.25
Eggs (6)	£0.68	Oil (1 litre)	£0.65	Tea (40 teabags)	£0.50
Coffee (100g)	£1.60	Sugar (2lb)	£0.54	Cereal (cornflakes)	£0.75
Yoghurt	£0.26	Margarine	£0.30	Nuts (small packet)	£0.25
Baby foods	£0.35	Tomatoes (1lb)	£0.52	Fruit juice (carton)	£0.98
Potatoes (1lb)	£0.14	Biscuits	£0.30	Soup (small can)	£0.25
Carrots (1lb)	£0.12	Cabbage	£0.30	Peas (frozen, 1lb)	£0.79
Apples (1lb)	£0.38	Onions (1lb)	£0.15	Mushrooms (1lb)	£0.40
Oranges (each)	£0.15	Steak (1lb)	£2.00	Green pepper (1lb)	£0.40
Bananas (1lb)	£1.03	Lamb (1lb)	£1.98	Chicken (1lb)	£0.88
Cheese (1lb)	£1.30–£2	Sausages	£0.95		

Books and stationery

Allow about £175–£350 per year for books and stationery (Postgraduate students should allow £300–£500 for the preparation of their thesis).

Childcare

Many universities and polytechnics run their own nurseries and
playgroups for the children of the students. These are usually free.
Alternatively, you can use:

Private nurseries	£30–£40 per week
State sector nurseries	£4–£30 (fee depends on parents' income)

There are very long waiting lists for both types of nursery. Some
people prefer to employ **childminders** or **babysitters**. These people
are often students themselves, who come to your house and look
after your child while you are out. Babysitters usually advertise
themselves in local newspapers, college noticeboards or newsagent
shop windows. For professional childminders, contact The National
Childminders Association, 8 Masons Hill, Bromley, Kent BR2 9EY.
Tel: (01) 464 6164.

The prices quoted in the various sections above are intended to give
you a *general idea* of the cost of living in Britain. It is your decision
how much you spend.

When you are a student, you will probably experience a lower
standard of living than usual. If you have to reduce your spending,
do it sensibly. Don't economise on heating, food and rent. Health
and environment are very important factors in your success as a
student. You cannot study if you are cold, unwell or living in very
uncomfortable accommodation.

Don't expect to be able to get a job to supplement your income.
Some students *may* be given permission to take part time or vacation
work, but it isn't easy to get a work permit. If you are attending all
your classes, you won't have enough time for a job. If you try to
combine day-time study with a night-time job you will find it hard to
cope and your studies may suffer as a result. Part time work should
be regarded as an emergency measure only.

SCHOLARSHIPS AND GRANTS

Some students can apply for a scholarship. There are four main
sources of scholarships for study in Britain:

● scholarships provided by the British government;
● scholarships provided by your own government or by an
  international organisation;
● sponsorship by British industry;
● sponsorship by industrial or commercial companies in your home
  country.

You can obtain details of all types of scholarships from either your local British Council office or from the Ministry of Education/Department of Education in your home country.

Different scholarships last for different periods of time, provide different amounts of money and have different conditions attached to them. It is very important to make sure that the scholarship you are applying for will meet your particular needs.

IMPORTANT POINTS TO CONSIDER WHEN APPLYING FOR A SCHOLARSHIP

- Make your application well in advance of wanting to begin a course. Applications can take up to one year to process.

- For every scholarship available, there are hundreds of other students applying for it. When you fill in the application form, make sure that it is neat and tidy and that you have provided all the information required. The way you present yourself on this form is very important.

- You will be given a scholarship in order to study a particular course. Once you have accepted the scholarship it is unlikely that you will be able to change course.

- Some scholarships have very strict conditions attached to them. One condition that you will almost always find is that you agree to return to your home country when you have finished the course.

- If you are being sponsored by a company, you will normally be required to work for them for a specified length of time after you have completed your course.

- Some scholarships will cover the cost of travel, tuition fees, living expenses, books and even clothes. Others will only cover the cost of the course fees. Make sure you know exactly what costs a scholarship covers before you apply for it.

- Make sure that the scholarship will last for the length of your course. Some scholarships only last for one year.

- You can only get a scholarship if you are a single student. It will not provide enough money to keep your wife/husband and any children you may have.

The following are some of the organisations and schemes which exist for students from overseas who want to apply for a scholarship.

British Council Fellowship Programme

The British Council offers scholarships to students from over seventy different countries. These scholarships can be used for a wide range of different courses at any level. Write to the British Council office or the British Embassy in your home country for details, or try The British Council, 10 Spring Gardens, London SW1A 2BN. Tel: (01) 930 8466.

Commonwealth Scholarship and Fellowship Plan

The scholarships are usually provided only for **research** or study at **postgraduate level**. They are open to students from commonwealth countries. The fellowships are available for **teachers** who wish to study at **postdoctorate** level.

You can obtain details from the Ministry of Education in your home country, or from the UK Commonwealth Scholarship Commission, John Foster House, 36 Gordon Square, London WC1H 0PF. Tel: (01) 387 8572.

Confederation of British Industry (CBI)

The CBI offers scholarships to students of **engineering** who wish to undergo a period of practical training. Details are available from your local British Council office.

Foreign and Commonwealth Office Scholarships and Awards Scheme

These scholarships are offered to students from a wide variety of countries. They allow you to study in any subject but study at **postgraduate level** is preferred. Details are available from The Cultural Relations Department, Foreign and Commonwealth Office, Old Admiralty Buildings, Whitehall, London SW1A 2AF. Tel: (01) 270 3000.

Foreign and Commonwealth Office Support Schemes

These offer scholarships for students from Malaysia, Hong Kong, Cyprus, Bermuda and Cayman Islands. The scholarships are normally awarded for study at first degree level or equivalent. Details are available from The Cultural Relations Department, Foreign and Commonwealth Office (address as above).

Hong Kong Shared Funding Scheme
This provides scholarships for students from Hong Kong who are
taking **full-time, first degree or equivalent** courses at a university or
any other public sector institution.
   Details are available from the Hong Kong government, or from
Overseas Student Policy Section, Cultural Relations Department, Old
Admiralty Building, London SW1A 2AF. Tel: (01) 270 3000.

Marshall Scholarships
These are scholarships available for students from The United States
of America, who are **under 26** years old and are studying at **first degree
level**. Details from Marshall Aid Commemoration Commission, 36
Gordon Square, London WC1H 0PF. Tel: (01) 387 8572.

Overseas Department Administration Scholarship Scheme
These scholarships cover the cost of tuition fees only and are available
for students from commonwealth countries who wish to study at a
university or polytechnic. Preference is given to **postgraduate** students,
and to those studying subjects relevant to the economic and social
development of their country. Details are available from the British
High Commission in your home country or from The Education
Department, Overseas Development Administration, Eland House,
Stag Place, London SW1E 5DH. Tel: (01) 213 3000.

Overseas Research Students Awards Scheme
This scheme provides only *part* of the tuition fees. The awards
are available for **postgraduate research** in any subject at certain
listed colleges. Details are available from The Committee of Vice-
Chancellors and Principals, 29 Tavistock Square, London WC1H
9EZ. Tel: (01) 387 9231.

Technical Co-operation and Training Programme
This programme offers scholarships for study at **postgraduate** level,
and preferably in subjects which will enable the candidates to
contribute to the economic, social and technical development of their
country. Candidates for these scholarships should be from *developing
countries* and should be *nominated by their own government*. Priority
is given to those who will return to their home country and be in a
position to pass on to others the knowledge and skills they have
obtained. Details are available from The Education Department,
Overseas Department Administration (address as above).

United Nations Educational, Scientific and Cultural Organisation (UNESCO)

UNESCO offers a variety of awards and scholarships. You can obtain details from UNESCO, 7 Place de Fontenoy, 75700 Paris, France.

You can obtain further information about scholarships for students from the books listed below. Most of these books should be available at your local British Council office. As they are only reference books, and most of them are very expensive, don't buy them unless you have no choice.

Study Abroad, UNESCO, 7 Place de Fontenoy, 75700 Paris, France *Or* HMSO, PO Box 276, London SW8 5DT.

Financial Aid for First Degree Study at Commonwealth Universities, ACU, 36 Gordon Square, London WC1H 0PF.

British Government and British Council Award Schemes for Overseas Students, Cultural Relations Department, Foreign and Commonwealth Office, Old Admiralty Building, Whitehall, London SW1A 2AF.

The Grants Register, Macmillan Publishers Ltd.

The Directory of Grant Making Trusts, Charities Aid Foundation, 48 Penbury Road, Tonbridge, Kent TN9 2JD.

Scholarship Guide for Commonwealth Postgraduate Students, ACU, 36 Gordon Square, London WC1H 0PF.

LOCAL EDUCATION AUTHORITY (LEA) GRANTS

LEA grants are awarded by the government. These grants are the main source of financial support for the majority of British students while they are at college. Most students from overseas will not be eligible for an LEA grant. In order to be eligible, you must satisfy three conditions.

● You must have been *ordinarily resident* in Britain for a *full three years* before:

1st September, if your course begins in the Autumn term; **or**
1st January, if your course begins in January; **or**
1st April, if your course begins in summer.

To be ordinarily resident means that you must live in Britain on a settled basis, and not be in Britain temporarily, as a student, a visitor or on holiday.

● During those three years, or for any part of those three years, you must *not* have been a full-time student.

● You must be enrolled on a **designated** course. That is one which appears on a list produced by the local education authority. Most of the designated courses are first degree courses.

There are some exceptions to these rules. Even if you do *not* fulfil the conditions above, you can *still* apply for an LEA grant if:

● you are a refugee, with refugee status given by the British Government;

● you are the child/wife/husband of a refugee;

● you have not been able to live in Britain for the required period of three years because your parents/husband/wife had a job abroad *for a temporary period only;*

● if you are from the **EC** (European Community) and you came to Britain originally for employment. In this case you must have been in Britain for at least one year and have been employed for nine months of that year. Also, the course you wish to take must be a vocational one.

● if you are the child of an EC worker currently employed in Britain, or the child of a retired EC worker who has been employed for at least one year during the previous three years.

The regulations concerning LEA grants are very complicated. If you are already living in Britain, and if you think you may be eligible for a LEA grant, contact:

— the local education authority in the area where you are living;
— the welfare officer or student union officer at your college.

If you cannot get help from either of these sources, or if your college does not have a welfare officer or student union, you can contact an organisation called **The United Kingdom Council For Overseas Student Affairs** (UKCOSA). See Appendix 2 for details.

FOREIGN EXCHANGE

Although there is no limit to the amount of money you can bring into Britain, don't carry large sums of money with you. The best way of getting large amounts of money to Britain is by **currency transfer.**

Methods of transferring currency
● Banker's draft
● International money order

- Cashier's cheque
- Telegraphic transfer

The first three on the list are basically the same. They are instructions from your own bank to credit a bank in Britain with an amount of money. You can either have this sent through the post, or you can bring it with you.

If you are having it sent you should first of all find out the **name**, **address** and **code number (sort code)** of a bank near to where you are going to study. Ask your college for this information. Some universities and polytechnics have branches of banks on their own premises. Don't forget to keep details of the bank and its address for when you arrive in Britain. Also keep details of the date the draft was sent and how much it was for.

If you decide to bring the draft with you, you will be able to cash it at any bank but it will take about ten days to **clear** (that means ten days before you have access to any of the money).

A **telegraphic transfer** is the quickest, safest but most expensive way of transferring money to Britain.

By this method, the money will be transferred to a bank of your choice in Britain, where you can collect it in cash or use it to open a bank account. Whichever method you choose, you need to take your passport for identification when you go to collect the money.

If money is going to be transferred to you at regular intervals, make sure that the person dealing with it understands:

- exactly how much they must transfer each month/term;
- where they are having it transferred to;
- how long the money will take to arrive in Britain, and by what date you need the money.

Foreign exchange controls

Some countries have laws concerning the transfer of money. These laws exist to limit the amounts of money which can be allowed out of the country.

Before you apply for a course, consult your own bank to find out:

- whether your country has foreign exchange control;
- if there is a maximum amount which can be transferred in any one year;
- if there are controls, what the procedures are for obtaining permission to transfer money and what documents you will require;
- what the regulations are concerning foreign exchange. For

example, some countries only allow foreign exchange for approved courses or colleges.

If you are on a government scholarship, it is unlikely that you will have any problems about obtaining permission to transfer money.

If you *do* have to obtain permission to transfer money, you will probably need to provide:
— evidence that you have a place on a course;
— evidence of how much the fees will be;
— (sometimes) written evidence from the institution of the amount of money required for living expenses.

Do not accept an offer of a place on a course until you are sure that your application for foreign exchange has been approved. Certainly do not travel to Britain unless you have applied for permission to transfer money and you are sure that your application has been approved.

If you know that students from your home country have experienced difficulties with foreign exchange and if you think that you may also have problems with foreign exchange, find out this information by asking the student union or the welfare officer at the college:

● If your money was delayed, would the college allow you to remain on the course, and for how long?
● If you were asked to leave, would you lose the money you had already paid?
● If you owed money to the college, would they prevent you from taking your examinations, or collecting your results?

TRAVEL INSURANCE

When you buy your ticket to travel, you can usually arrange travel insurance for yourself and your luggage at the same time. Don't travel without **travel insurance**. If you are unlucky and lose your luggage, the cost of replacing everything will use up a lot of the money you had brought with you. While you are packing your luggage, make a list of the contents of each suitcase, just in case it is lost and you have to claim insurance.

If it is the airline which loses your luggage, *do not* hand in your baggage claim ticket (this is usually attached to your travel ticket). It will probably take some time to get full compensation from the airline, but you can ask for **spot compensation**, which will provide you with some money to buy things you need immediately.

MONEY FOR YOUR JOURNEY

Carry with you a small amount of cash in **sterling** (British currency) for use on your journey and for when you first arrive at your destination. About £100 should be enough, but you will need more if you need to travel a long distance between your point of arrival and your final destination (see travel prices on page 50).

If you didn't have your money sent to Britain long enough before your arrival, or if you are carrying a cheque or banker's draft with you (see page 62), then also bring some **travellers cheques** to use while you are waiting for your cheque or draft to clear. This can take up to two weeks.

It is safer to carry travellers cheques than large amounts of cash. They can be cashed into small amounts when you need the money. When you buy your travellers cheques, write down the **serial numbers** of the cheques. Keep this information in a safe place, separate from the cheques themselves, in case you lose them.

BEFORE YOU TRAVEL — A MONEY CHECKLIST

● Do you know what rate of fees the college is going to charge you?

● Do you know what the fees include and what they do not include?

● Have you calculated your living expenses for the whole time you will be in Britain?

● Have you enough money to pay the fees and your living expenses for the duration of the course?

● Are you eligible for any form of scholarship?

● How and when does the college require the fees to be paid?

● Have you checked whether your country has foreign exchange controls? If so, have you obtained permission to transfer money?

● Have you arranged for a sum of money to be sent to Britain well in advance of your own arrival?

● Have you arranged for someone to make regular payments of money from your bank to a bank in Britain?

- Have you ordered enough travellers cheques and a small amount of British currency, for your first few days in Britain?

- Have you bought your travel tickets and travel insurance?

CHANGING MONEY

Once you have arrived in Britain, you can change money or cash travellers cheques at any bank or Bureau de Change. To cash travellers cheques, you need your passport for identification.

If you have not brought any British currency with you, obtain some *before* you leave the airport, where there is a 24-hour bank. Most other banks in Britain are open **only between 9.30am and 3.30pm, Monday to Friday.**

Bureaux de Change are open for longer hours than banks and also on Saturdays and Sundays. They will, however, charge you a fee for cashing cheques and their exchange rates are not usually as favourable as those at a bank.

British currency consists of **notes** (paper money) and **coins**. The coins available are worth **1p (pence), 2p, 5p, 10p, 20p, 50p, £1 (100p) and £2.** The notes available are worth **£5 (blue notes), £10 (brown notes), £20 (purple notes) and £50 (green/brown notes).**

OPENING A BANK ACCOUNT

When you arrive at your final destination, open a bank account as soon as possible at a bank near to your college.

To open a current account, you need to provide the names and addresses of two **referees**. These should be two people you know who have a bank account in Britain.

There are many different types of bank account available. The two which would be of most use to you, as a student, are described below. You can choose one or the other or even have both types of account.

Deposit account

A deposit account is like a savings account. The money you have in the account earns you **interest**, that is, money paid to you while your savings are in the bank.

If you have an account which earns interest, you must inform the bank that you are from overseas and they will ask you to complete a **declaration of non-residence form**. Otherwise, you will have to pay tax on the interest you receive.

There are many different kinds of deposit accounts available. Some provide you with a cheque book, others do not. Investigate several banks before deciding on the type of account which is best for you.

If you plan to open a savings account, always check how many days' **notice** (warning) you must give before you can withdraw your money, otherwise you may not be able to get at it when you really need it.

Current account

If you open a current account you are given a **cheque book** and, eventually, a **cheque card**. You will have to wait for a few weeks for your cheque card.

Use of cheque book, without card	*Use of cheque book, with card*
● Withdraw money from your bank but only at the branch where you have your account (no limit).	● Withdraw money from any branch of the bank which has your account (up to a limit of £50).
	● Use cheques to pay for purchases in shops (up to a limit of £50).

In theory, you can withdraw money (with a cheque card) and pay money into your account at any bank. However, if it is not the bank which has your account, you will be charged a fee (£3–£6) for each transaction.

Cashpoint cards

Cashpoint cards are very useful items. They allow you to get money from machines built into the wall outside your bank and they can be used when the bank itself is closed.

The bank usually sends you a cashpoint card soon after you open your account. A few days later, they will send you your **personal identification number** which you must learn. You will need the number every time you use card.

Overdrafts

To have an overdraft means that you have taken more money from your account than was in it. In other words, you are borrowing money from the bank.

There are two types of overdraft:

- One which has been **authorised** (which means you have asked the bank manager for permission to overdraw your account for a limited period of time).

- One which is **unauthorised** (which is when you overdraw your account without asking permission. It is impossible to do this if you do not have a cheque card.).

If possible, *try to avoid any kind of overdraft*. Once you have got yourself in debt it is very difficult to put it right. If you spend too much money one month, you may feel that you can easily pay it back from next month's money, but then you will be short of money that month, and so on.

Overdrafts are also expensive. You are charged interest on the money you are borrowing from the bank, and you are also charged a fee each time you withdraw or pay money into your account during the time you are overdrawn. The charges for an unauthorised overdraft are higher than those for an authorised overdraft.

Building societies

Traditionally, **building societies** have offered only savings accounts. Now they have started to offer current accounts, and they are becoming more popular as alternatives to banks. Their current accounts work in exactly the same way as a bank current account, with cheque books and cheque cards and so on. The difference between them is that, unlike many bank current accounts, a building society pays you interest on the money you have in your account. Building societies also offer a wide range of savings accounts.

INSURANCE POLICIES

If you have any valuables, for example, jewellery or camera equipment, take out a **policy** to **insure** these items in case they are lost or stolen while you are in Britain. Two companies which offer a special insurance policy for students are:

- Endsleigh Insurance Services, Endsleigh House, Cheltenham, Gloucestershire GL50 3NR. Tel: (0242) 36151;
- Harrison Beaumont Ltd, 4 Meadow Court High Street, Whitney, Oxfordshire OX8 6LP. Tel: (0993) 703251.

There are two types of policy available, so make sure you get the one you want. A **new-for-old** policy will pay you the full cost of buying new replacements for your possessions if they are lost or stolen. An **indemnity** policy will only pay you the second-hand value of your possessions. The amount you are paid will depend on how old each item was. Indemnity policies are cheaper than new-for-old policies.

BUDGETING AND MANAGING MONEY

For some people, this may be the first time away from home and the first time you have had to organise your own money.

When you arrive in Britain, you will probably have a lot of money in your bank account. This may make you feel suddenly rich, and you may be tempted to go out and spend some of it. *Don't forget that it has got to last you for a whole term, three to four months, or even a whole year.*

There are various ways of managing your money. Eventually you will find a way which suits you, but you can try the plan on page 70 to start off with. The plan assumes that you will be in Britain for a year.

When you have found out what your weekly allowance is, make a list of all the *essentials* which you have to buy each week (food, travel, books and so on). When you have calculated the weekly cost of essentials, you will be able to see how much you have left each week for general spending money.

It will probably take you several weeks to get used to living according to a tight budget. For the first few weeks it might be a good idea to write down *everything* you spend in one week. If this total is more than your weekly spending allowance then you are spending too much and must find somewhere to make cuts.

Don't forget, however, that during your first few weeks at a new college, you will probably spend more money than at any other time. For example, you'll buy new books, stationery, maybe some new clothes and, just as important, spend money on going out and getting to know people. A full social life can be very expensive.

Don't be tempted by credit cards and credit schemes in shops, which allow you to buy now and pay later. Using any form of credit is an expensive way of buying things as the interest charged is very high.

Paying bills

If you are living in private accommodation, you will probably have to pay gas bills, electricity bills and telephone bills.

These bills come every **quarter**, which means every three months. With gas and electricity, there will be a **meter** — a machine to record

How much money can I spend each week?

1. *Add up your income for one year.* This may be an amount being sent to you every month, or an amount you have brought with you, or have had sent over in advance. **TOTAL A**

2. *Pay the following bills,* if they have not been paid in advance;
   - your school or college fees (most colleges will require fees for the whole year to be paid when you enrol);
   - any other amounts required by the college, for example deposits (see page 48);
   - if you are living in college accommodation, pay for your accommodation for one year in advance. If you are not living in college accommodation, calculate your rent for a whole term (even if you only have to pay weekly or monthly). Put the amount into a savings account and leave it there until your rent needs to be paid. **TOTAL B**

3. *Subtract* TOTAL B *from* TOTAL A.
   This will show you how much money you have left, once the most important items have been paid for. **TOTAL C**

4. *Take from* TOTAL C *an amount to set aside,* to cover any long term expenses you may have, for example:
   - end of year examination fees
   - having your thesis typed up
   - art materials, science equipment
   - money for gas and electricity bills for the year (if you are not living in college accommodation)
   - money for your fare home. Even if your have a return ticket don't forget you need money to get to the airport

   This money for long term expenses should, if possible, be put away in a savings account where it can be making interest until you need it. This will be easy to do if you have come to Britain with money for the whole year in advance. If you are having money sent over every month, you should calculate a fixed amount to save every month for these long term expenses.

   When you have subtracted your long term expenses from TOTAL C you now have a new total which is for your day-to-day living expenses. **TOTAL D**

5. *Divide* TOTAL D *by the number of weeks in the year.*
   This will give you the amount you have for spending each week.

the amount you use — in your house or flat. About a week before you receive your bill, someone will come round to the house to **read the meter**. If you are not in at the time they will probably make an estimate based on how much gas or electricity was used the previous quarter.

Because you don't pay these bills every month or every week, their total may come as a surprise to you. The cost of gas and electricity in Britain is probably much higher than in your home country. Also, if you come from a hot country you will probably be using large amounts of gas and electricity for heating, particularly in winter. Put aside a small amount of money each week or each month so that you will have saved enough money to pay the bill when it arrives.

If you share a telephone with other people, everyone should agree to pay for their calls as they make them, by putting the right amount of money into a box next to the phone, or by writing down in a book the cost of the call they have just made.

It is very important to pay bills on time, within about two weeks of receiving them. Otherwise, you will be **cut off**. This means that your supply of gas or electricity will be stopped, or your telephone line disconnected. It is expensive to be reconnected.

There are several ways to pay your bills, and these are explained on the bill itself. The easiest way is to pay at a post-office.

Poll tax

Poll tax, sometimes referred to as the **community charge,** is being introduced into Britain to replace the system of paying **rates** (a payment towards such services as schools, police, maintenance of roads and pavements, waste disposal). This is unfortunate for students. Homeowners were the only people who paid rates, but everyone will have to pay poll tax.

At the moment, poll tax only affects students who are at schools and colleges in Scotland. Students in the rest of Britain will probably have to pay poll tax after April, 1990. Students who are from overseas will have to pay a reduced poll tax, which is about 20% of the full rate. This will be about £65 per year for each adult.

If you have any doubts about paying poll tax, talk to the welfare officer or student union at your college, or go to a local Citizens Advice Bureau.

FINANCIAL PROBLEMS

Even if you are well prepared, you can still easily have financial problems when you are in Britain — for example, because of:

- an unstable political situation in your home country;
- foreign exchange problems;
- a changed personal situation.

If you are suffering from financial problems, do the following:

1. Inform your **Embassy** or **High Commission**. They may be able to help you, particularly if you are having problems with foreign exchange.

2. Don't keep the problem to yourself. Go to a **welfare officer, the student union** or a **tutor** at your college. First of all they will be able to tell you what you should do about paying your fees. The college *may* allow you to delay payment for a short time, or accept payment in instalments.

    Some institutions have something called a **hardship fund**, for students who are having severe financial problems. Others may provide you with a short term loan. They should also be able to advise you about the best place to go for help.

3. Apply to one of the **charities** or trusts listed on page 73. Some private charities only consider your application if you have tried all other sources of help.

4. Apply for a state benefit called **Income Support**.

The Income Support scheme

Under regulation 70(3)a of the **Income Support scheme**, students from overseas can, during any one period of stay in Britain, obtain money for a maximum of six weeks. As claims under this regulation of the Income Support scheme are *not* regarded by the Home Office as *recourse to public funds*, making such a claim will *not* affect your right to remain in Britain. You can make a claim if the following conditions apply to you:

- you have previously supported yourself, and any dependants you may have, without recourse to public funds;
- you are *temporarily* without money;
- there is a good chance that your financial situation will improve quite soon.

If you decide to make a claim, **contact an adviser** first, as you may need help making your claim. You can also phone (0800) 393 555 for information. The phone call is free and it avoids having to queue up for hours at a local social security office.

Other state benefits
One of the conditions of being allowed to enter, and to remain in, Britain is that you do not have recourse to public funds (see page 77). This means *not* claiming state benefits. However, recourse to public funds has been defined as making claims for:

— Housing Benefit;
— Housing under the 1985 Act;
— Family Credit and Income Support.

This means that the only other state benefit you can claim is **Child Benefit**.

You can claim child benefit if you have a dependent child or children and if you have been in Britain for at least six months (anyone from the EC can claim as soon as they arrive in Britain).

Information about child benefit can be found on leaflets **CB1** and **CB2**, which can be obtained from your local Social Security office (the address can be found in a telephone directory but don't look under 's' for social as it is listed under 'd' for Department of Health and Social Security, or simply Department of Social Security.

What not to do if you have financial problems
If you are suffering from financial hardship:

● don't try to apply for a work permit;
● don't get a job without a work permit;
● don't try to become a part time student;
● don't ignore bills or letters from college demanding fees;
● don't keep the problem to yourself;
● don't go to a loan agency, they charge a very high rate of interest;
● don't worry.

TRUSTS AND CHARITIES

There are a few trusts and charities which help students who are in temporary financial difficulty. However, these organisations only offer very small amounts of money and usually only help students who are near to the end of their course.

Each organisation has its own rules and criteria. For example, some only give money to students who are following courses in science subjects, some only help female students, some are limited to students from certain countries. Check to see if you qualify, before making an application, otherwise you will be wasting time, effort and you will end up being disappointed. The major trusts are:

— **The Africa Educational Trust,** The Africa Centre, 38 King Street, London WC2E 8JT. Tel: (01) 836 5075. This trust makes *small* grants to *African* students who are in temporary difficulty and close to the end of their course.

— **The Barrow and Geraldine Cadbury Trust,** The Assistant Secretary, 2 College Walk, Selly Oak, Birmingham B29 6LE. Tel: (021) 472 0417. This trust awards grants to students who are studying in the *West Midlands* only. Applications are not accepted directly from students. Someone from your college must apply on your behalf.

— **The Lee Foundation,** Malaysian Students Department, 44 Bryanston Square, London W1H 8AS. Tel: (01) 723 2265. This trust gives very small grants to students from *Malaysia*. The grants are only available to students who are in their final year of studies.

— **The Sino-British Fellowship Trust,** c/o Honorary Secretary, Buchanan House, 20–30 Holborn, London EC1 2PX. This trust provides grants for *postgraduate* students from the *Far East*.

— **The World University Service,** 20 Compton Terrace, London N1 2UN. Tel: (01) 226 6747. This trust provides money for students from *developing countries and third world countries*, if the financial problem is a result of an unstable political situation in the student's home country. The World University Service also provides financial aid for students who are refugees.

— **Educational Grants Advisory Service,** c/o Family Welfare Association, 501/505 Kingsland Road, London E8 4AU. Tel: (01) 254 6251. This organisation does *not* provide money. It exists to advise students in difficulty and to put them in touch with sources of financial help.

FOREIGN EXCHANGE — WHAT MAY HAVE GONE WRONG

Even though you made all the necessary arrangements and obtained approval for foreign exchange before you left home, you may find that money is not coming through for a variety of reasons. For example:

- Your sponsor, or whoever is responsible for your money, has not deposited the money in the bank back home;
- There are administrative problems;
- There isn't enough money at the Central Bank;
- Instructions from one bank to another have been delayed;
- The money has been sent to the wrong bank in Britain.

If you find that money you had expected has not arrived:

1. Check with your **sponsor**, or whoever is responsible for your money, that the money was deposited in the bank.
2. Contact the **Central Bank** in your home country, or its British branch if there is one, and find out when the money was transferred to Britain and which bank it was transferred to.
3. Contact your **High Commission** or Embassy for help.

If you are having problems with foreign exchange, you *must* inform your college, so they know that there is a *valid* reason why your fees are not being paid.

DEBT COUNSELLING

If you do get yourself into bad debt, you should go to a **debt counsellor** who can help you to control your spending before you get into worse debt. Your student union or local Citizens Advice Bureau will be able to help you. A debt counsellor will help you to cope with your debts by organising a practical plan of action.

They will help you to **prioritise** your debts; this means that you decide which debts you should pay first. For example, money owing to the gas or electricity company is usually the most important as your supply of light or heating might be cut off.

They will then help you to negotiate agreements with each of your *creditors*, the people you owe money to, so that you can pay off a realistic amount each week. Once the amount has been fixed, you *must* keep to it. Finally, they will show you where you can make cuts in your spending and how to avoid going further into debt.

4
The United Kingdom Immigration Rules

Before you make any arrangements to travel to Britain and before you pay any school or college fees, you must make sure that you will be able to enter Britain and stay for the duration of your course.

What you must do before you can enter Britain
Anyone from any country which does *not* belong to the EC, must obtain **entry clearance**.

What is entry clearance?
There are three different types of entry clearance.

1. Visa
2. Entry certificate
3. Letter of consent

Where to obtain entry clearance
To obtain entry clearance, go to the nearest British Embassy or High Commission or Consulate in your home country. The process of obtaining entry clearance can take some time, so apply a long time before you want to come to Britain if possible.

What it will cost
All forms of entry clearance cost £20 (in 1989).

The documents you need
Before giving you entry clearance, the Entry Clearance Officer must be satisfied that you meet the requirements of the United Kingdom immigration rules which relate to students. These requirements are as follows:

● that you have been accepted for a course of study at a university, polytechnic or a *bona fide* (genuine) college or school;

- **that you will be occupied** for the whole, or most of your time in full-time study. This is defined as no less than fifteen hours per week of organised *day-time* study;
- **that you can support yourself** and any dependants you may have, without working or without recourse to public funds (claiming state benefits);
- **that the qualifications you have are adequate** for the course you intend to follow;
- **that you intend to leave Britain** when you have completed your studies.

The Entry Clearance Officer will usually ask you to complete a form and then will interview you. You should be able to produce documents to prove you meet the requirements listed above. Your documents should be originals and not photocopies.

For example:
- A letter from the school or college.
- Certificates of the qualifications you hold.
- Recent bank statements or a letter from your bank.
- Evidence of financial support if you are not supporting yourself — for example, a sponsor's letter or confirmation of a scholarship.

What can you do if you are not yet enrolled at a college?

Perhaps you want to travel to Britain *before* you have enrolled at a school or college. You may wish to look round at a few different colleges before making your final decision. In this case:

- You **must** explain your intentions to the entry clearance officer.
- Do not try to travel to Britain as a tourist if your real intention is to study.

If the officer is satisfied that you *do* intend to study when you have found a suitable college, and if you fulfil all the other immigration requirements, then he will give you a special kind of entry clearance. When you arrive in Britain you will be given permission to enter and stay for a short period of time (usually about two months), so that you can find a college and enrol there. When you have organised everything you can then apply for an extension of your stay.

What can you do if your application for entry clearance is refused?

If the Entry Clearance Officer is not satisfied that you meet the requirements of the immigration regulations, he can refuse your application for entry clearance.

He will give you reasons for the refusal, in writing, and instructions on how to make an appeal against the decision. You **must** make your appeal within three months of the date of the refusal.

Does entry clearance guarantee entry into Britain?

No, entry clearance does not *guarantee* entry into Britain, but it makes entering Britain much easier.

When you arrive in Britain you will still have to pass through immigration control and answer the questions of the immigration officer. The immigration officer can refuse to give you permission to stay but he must have special reasons for doing so.

If you are not given permission to stay in Britain, entry clearance does guarantee you the right to appeal against this decision and to remain in Britain until the appeal has been heard.

What will happen if you travel to Britain without entry clearance?

If you travel to Britain *without* an entry clearance you *may* be allowed to enter, but the immigration officer will certainly ask alot of questions. You will need to be able to show that you meet all the immigration requirements listed on page 76. If you are refused entry you could be returned *immediately* to your home country. You will have wasted alot of time and money. You *can* appeal against the decision to refuse you entry but *only after you have left Britain*. The time limit for making this appeal is twenty-eight days. The appeal is dealt with in Britain but you will not be able to be present at the hearing.

Dependants — wife/husband, children

If you are male and you wish to bring your wife and any children (under 18), you must also obtain entry clearance for them. You must prove that you can support them as well as yourself. You must also prove that you are married by showing a certificate of marriage. The wife and children of a male student will be free to work or to study, either full-time or part-time. They will usually be given permission to stay in Britain for the same length of time as you.

If you are female, you cannot bring your husband with you. He must obtain entry clearance for himself in the same way as you, for example, by being a full-time student or by coming to Britain as a tourist.

Which type of entry clearance will I need?

Country of Origin	Form of Entry Clearance Required
Afghanistan, Albania, Angola, Argentina, Bangladesh, Benin, Bhutan, Bulgaria, Burma, Burundi, Cameroon, Comoros, Cape Verdi, Central African Republic, Chad, China, Congo, Cuba, Czechoslovakia, Djibouti, Egypt, Equatorial Guinea, Ethiopia, Gabon, Germany (Democratic Republic), Ghana, Guinea, Guinea-Bissau, Haiti, Hungary, India, Indonesia, Iran, Iraq, Jordan, Kampuchea, Korea, Laos, Lebanon, Liberia, Libya, Madagascar, Mali, Mauritania, Mongolia, Mozambique, Nepal, Nigeria, Oman, Pakistan, Philippines, Poland, Rumania, Rwanda, Soa Tome e Principe, Saudi Arabia, Senegal, Somali Democratic Republic, Soviet Union, Sri Lanka, Sudan, Syria, Thailand, Togo, Turkey, Burkina, Vietnam, Yemen, Zaire.	VISA
Anguilla, Antigua, Ascension, Australia, Bahamas, Barbados, Barbuda, Belize, Botswana, Brunei, Canada, Cayman Islands, Cyprus, Dominica, Falklands, Fiji, Gambia, Gilbert and Ellice Islands, Grenada, Grenadines, Guyana, Hong Kong, Indonesia, Jamaica, Kenya, Kiribati, Leeward Islands, Lesotho, Malawi, Malaysia, Malta, Mauritius, Montserrat, Nauru, New Hebrides, New Zealand, Papua New Guinea, St Helena, St Lucia, St Vincent, St Christopher, St Kitts and Nevis, Samoa, Seychelles, Sierra Leone, Sikkim, Singapore, Solomon Islands, Swaziland, Tanzania, Tongo, Trinidad and Tobago, Tristan da Cunha, Tuvalu, Uganda, Vanuata, Virgin Islands, Western Samoa, Zambia, Zimbabwe.	ENTRY CERTIFICATE
All other countries (including Spain and Portugal until January 1993)	LETTER OF CONSENT
EC countries: Belgium, Denmark, Eire, France, Greece, Italy, Luxembourg, The Netherlands, West Germany.	NO ENTRY CLEARANCE REQUIRED
Students from EC countries may enter Britain freely for a period of six months. If after six months you wish to stay in Britain, you must extend your leave to remain by applying for a residence permit.	

Sample letter of consent

IMMIGRATION ACT 1971
LETTER OF CONSENT

Surname or family name

1. Miller
2. Miller (formerly Jones)
3. Miller

Forenames

1. James
2. Anne
3. Michael

Sex

1. Male
2. Female
3. Male

Nationality

1. United States citizen
2. United States citizen
3. United States citizen

Date of birth

1. 19.08.1951
2. 08.10.1954
3. 06.02.1982

Place of birth

1. Albany, Georgia, USA
2. Paris, France
3. New York, USA

Purpose of entry

1. Independent means
2. Accompanying husband
3. Accompanying father

Dear Mr Miller

You have applied for consent to the entry into the United Kingdom of the three persons described in the margin of this letter. I am pleased to inform you that the Secretary of State has agreed to this. The entry of the persons named will be facilitated if this letter is presented to an Immigration Officer on arrival at a United Kingdom port. The original must be presented and it is important that no alteration or amendment be made to it. A copy is not a valid entry clearance. In addition to this letter the persons named will require a valid passport or travel document.

On arrival in the United Kingdom the Immigration Officer will probably ask some questions and there are circumstances in which he may refuse leave to enter, but if he takes this exceptional course the reason will be given and there will be an entitlement to appeal immediately to an independent adjudicator.

This letter is valid if presented to an Immigration Officer within six months of its date. If it is not required for any reason it should be returned to this office.

Yours sincerely

H.O. ....

Embossing or
Authenticating Stamp   Frank Crawford

Crown copyright. Reproduced with the permission of the Controller of Her Majesty's Stationery Office.

Sample visas

Single entry   *Multiple entry*

Seen at the British Embassy

[Place]

Good for a single journey to

....

within three months of date
hereof, if passport remains
valid.

....

(Signed) ....

Date ....

Seen at the British Embassy

[Place]

Good for journeys to the United
Kingdom within six months of
date hereof, if passport remains
valid.

....

(Signed) ....

Date ....

Sample Entry Certificate

Crown copyright. Reproduced with the permission of
the Controller of Her Majesty's Stationery Office.

BEFORE TRAVELLING TO BRITAIN — AN IMMIGRATION CHECKLIST

- Make sure that your passport is not due to expire. If it is, apply for a new one.
- Obtain a letter from a college, proving that you have been unconditionally accepted onto a course.
- Obtain proof of finance (either a letter from your sponsor or recent bank statements).

- Find out whether or not you require entry clearance (visa, letter of consent, entry certificate) to come to Britain.

- If you do, make an application for entry clearance at the British Embassy or High Commission in your home country.

- If your application for entry clearance is refused, apply for an appeal and, in the meantime, collect any further documentation you may need to support your case.

ARRIVING IN BRITAIN — PASSPORT CONTROL

Whether you arrive in Britain by air or by sea, the first thing you will have to do when you land is go through **passport control**.

There are three different queues of people going through passport control:

— British passport holders
— EC nationals
— all other passport holders

Join the right queue. If you don't, you could waste a lot of time. Have all your documents (originals, not copies) and papers ready to show to the Immigration Officer. When it is your turn, he will ask you to show:

- your passport;
- a valid visa, entry certificate or letter of consent;
- a letter from your college providing evidence that you have been accepted on a full-time (15 hours per week) course of study;
- evidence that you can pay your fees and will be able to support yourself, and any dependants you might have with you, without working.
- evidence that you have obtained permission for foreign exchange, if you need it.

If you have not yet enrolled at a college, but you intend to study in Britain, *you must say so*. Do not try to enter as a tourist if you are really planning to study. If you enter as a tourist, you will have problems later on when you want to extend your permission to stay.

PROBLEMS AT PASSPORT CONTROL

Problems *may* occur if the Immigration Officer suspects that:
- you are not coming to Britain to study;

- you are not capable of following the course of study for which you are enrolled;
- your English is not of a high enough standard to allow you to follow the course (this does not apply if you are enrolled on an English language course);
- you do not have enough money to pay for your fees or to support yourself and any dependants you have with you;
- you do not intend to leave at the end of your studies;
- you obtained your entry clearance by deception, or that your circumstances have changed since you obtained it.

DOs and DON'Ts at passport control

Try not to say anything which would lead the Immigration Officer to doubt any of these things. For example;

If you are asked...	Don't Say...
...what do you intend to do when you have finished your course?	...that you would like to stay in Britain to get a job.
...do you think that Britain is a nice country and wouldn't you like to live here permanently?	...yes. (Don't be polite, *say no*.)

If you are asked...	Do say...
...anything about your future plans.	...that you are planning to get a job in your home country when you have finished your studies.
...whether you are intending to take another course after the first one?	...yes, if you are. Otherwise you may have difficulty getting permission to extend the length of your stay when you need to. But be clear and definite. Don't talk about lots of different courses which you may take later on.

If the Immigration Officer decides not to give you permission to enter Britain, what happens next depends on whether or not you had obtained entry clearance before you left your home country (See the table opposite).

UKIAS offices at ports of entry:

Heathrow airport	(01) 759 9234
Gatwick airport	(0293) 33385
Birmingham airport	(021) 706 9765
Manchester airport	(061) 834 9942
Folkestone and Dover Sea ports	(0303) 57829
Head office (London)	(01) 357 6917

(The numbers in brackets () are not needed if you are phoning from that particular airport or port).

Waiting for an appeal to be heard in Britain

If you have been allowed into Britain until your appeal has been heard, and as the appeal process can take quite a long time, sometimes several months, begin your course while you are waiting for the result. Otherwise you will miss your classes and will have a lot of catching up to do. However, talk to your college about paying fees. Find out if you can pay the fees in small amounts at a time, perhaps each month, just in case you lose the appeal and have to leave Britain.

Temporary admission

If you did not have entry clearance, instead of being asked to leave Britain, you *may* be given **temporary admission**. This means that, although you still have no right of appeal, you can remain in Britain until a decision has been made. The immigration authorities can grant temporary admission for as little as 24 hours, or for several weeks.

If this happens, the Immigration Officer will give you a time and a date to report back to him. You must also:

● provide the Immigration Officer with the address of the place where you will be staying, and *do not move from there*;
● hand your passport over to the Immigration Officer;
● use the time to find all the evidence you have been asked to produce (for example, evidence of having enough money, evidence that you have been accepted on a course).

If, at the end of the period of temporary admission, you have not been able to produce the required evidence, and all efforts to help you have failed, you must leave Britain.

What action can you take if you are refused entry into Britain?

You have entry clearance

1. You cannot be removed from Britain. You will be allowed to remain until your appeal has been heard.

2. You will be given the reasons for the refusal, in writing. You will also be told how to make an appeal against the decision.

3. Contact one of the following *immediately.*

   ● The United Kingdom Immigrants Advisory Council (UKIAS). Tel: (01) 357 6917;

   ● United Kingdom Council for Overseas Student Affairs (UKCOSA). Tel: (01) 229 9268.

4. They will be able to help you to make your appeal.

5. Contact your college to inform them what has happened.

You have no entry clearance

1. You will be asked to return *immediately* to your home country, or you will be given a very short period of **temporary admission** (see page 84).

2. If either of these things happen, contact the UKIAS office at your port of entry (numbers on page 85). *Do nothing until you have been advised by UKIAS.* They may be able to make special representations to stop your removal.

3. If special representations fail, leave Britain voluntarily. If you refuse to leave, you may be deported which would mean that you may have problems trying to enter Britain in the future.

4. Contact your college to inform them what has happened.

5. If you return to your home country, you can then make an appeal against the refusal (within 28 days). You cannot make an appeal while you are still in Britain.

LEAVE TO REMAIN IN BRITAIN

Hopefully, you will not have any of these problems and the Immigration Officer will be satisfied that you meet the requirements of the immigration regulations.

If this is the case, he will put a stamp in your passport.

The stamp will give you three pieces of information:

- how long you can remain in Britain (referred to as your **leave to remain**);
- whether you can apply for permission to work (see Chapter 9 for details);
- whether or not you need to register with the police (see Chapter 6).

You will probably be given leave to remain in Britain, as a student, for twelve months, unless you are enrolled on a very short course. Don't worry if you need more than twelve months. You will be able to extend your leave to remain later.

If you have not yet enrolled at a college, you will probably be given leave to remain for about two months. During this time you must choose a college and organise your study arrangements, then apply for an extension of your stay.

If you are unsure about *anything* which has been stamped in your passport, contact the student advisor or student union, as soon as you arrive at the college. If your college does not have a student advisor or student union, contact UKCOSA (see Appendix 2).

HOW THE IMMIGRATION RULES AFFECT YOU ONCE YOU ARE IN BRITAIN

It is very important to remember the date which appears on the stamp which has been put in your passport. This is when your current leave to remain finishes.

By this date you must have either:

- left Britain, or
- extended your leave to remain

If you stay in Britain after your current leave to remain has expired, you are committing a **criminal offence** and could be fined £200 or sent to prison.

EXTENDING YOUR LEAVE TO REMAIN

If you want to stay longer in Britain, you must apply for an extension

Samples of stamps which you may be given

Limited leave to enter with restriction on taking employment and requirement to register with the police.

Leave to enter the United Kingdom, on condition that the holder does not enter or change employment paid or unpaid without the consent of the Secretary of State for Employment, and does not engage in any business or profession without the consent of the Secretary of State for the Home Department, is hereby given for/until

....

IMMIGRATION OFFICER
✳ (790) ✳
27 NOV 1979
HEATHROW (3)

The holder is also required to register at once with the police.

Limited leave to enter with prohibition on taking employment and no requirement to register with the police.

Leave to enter the United Kingdom, on condition that the holder does not enter employment paid or unpaid and does not engage in any business or profession, is hereby given for/until

....

IMMIGRATION OFFICER
✳ (790) ✳
27 NOV 1979
HEATHROW (3)

Limited leave to enter with no restrictions on taking employment and no requirement to register with the police.

Leave the United Kingdom is hereby given for/until

....

IMMIGRATION OFFICER
✳ (790) ✳
27 NOV 1979
HEATHROW (3)

Limited leave to enter on a visit with prohibition on taking employment

LEAVE TO ENTER FOR SIX MONTHS EMPLOYMENT PROHIBITED

IMMIGRATION OFFICER
✳ (790) ✳
27 NOV 1979
HEATHROW (3)

of your leave to remain. Make the application about *six weeks* before your current leave expires, that is, six weeks before the date stamped in your passport. If you apply for your extension *after* this date, then:

● the Home Office will probably refuse to extend your leave to remain, unless you have a very good reason for making a late application;
● you will lose your right to appeal, if your application is refused;
● you will be committing a criminal offence.

Applications to extend your leave to remain can be made either **in writing** or **in person** (see page 93).

If, for any reason, you do not have all the required documents available when you need to extend your leave to remain, *do not delay making your application.* You must make your application on time. In this case, send the documents you have and enclose a letter which explains why certain documents are missing, and that you will send the remaining documents as soon as possible.

Late applications

If, for a very good reason, you can't make your application for an extension of your stay before your current leave to remain expires, you can make a **late application.** If you have to do this, you *must* seek advice from either the welfare officer at your college or from one of the organisations listed in Appendix 2.

Do not make a late application without first obtaining help and advice.

If you make a late application, try to get a letter from your college which states the following:

● the reason why your application was late:
● details of the course you are following;
● details of your record of attendance (if it is good);
● why they recommend that you should be given an extension of your leave to remain.

In addition to this letter, you must send all the required documents listed on page 93, with your application. It is advisable to make late applications by post and not in person.

If you are unsure about anything which relates to making an application for an extension of your leave to remain, contact either the welfare officer at your college or one of the organisations listed in Appendix 2.

Finally, when you receive an extension of your leave to remain you will find a stamp in your passport which looks like one of these:

Leave to remain in the United Kingdom, on condition that the holder does not engage in or change employment paid or unpaid without the consent of the Secretary of State for Employment, and does not engage in any business or profession without the consent of the Secretary of State for the Home Department is hereby given

until ....

....
on behalf of the Secretary of State
Home Office

Date ....

HOME OFFICE
IND
31 FEB 1984
(346)
IMMIG & NAT. DEPARTMENT

Leave to remain in the United Kingdom is hereby given

until ....

....
on behalf of the Secretary of State
Home Office

Date ....

HOME OFFICE
IND
31 FEB 1984
(346)
IMMIG & NAT. DEPARTMENT

Crown copyright. Reproduced with the permission of the Controller of Her Majesty's Stationery Office.

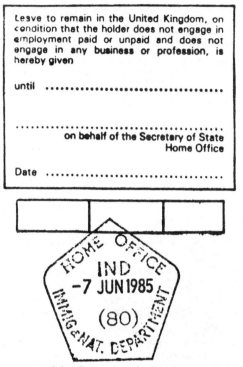

Leave to remain in the United Kingdom, on condition that the holder does not engage in employment paid or unpaid and does not engage in any business or profession, is hereby given

until ....

....
on behalf of the Secretary of State
Home Office

Date ....

HOME OFFICE
IND
-7 JUN 1985
(80)
IMMIG & NAT. DEPARTMENT

Crown copyright. Reproduced with the permission of
the Controller of Her Majesty's Stationery Office.

Students from EC countries

When you arrived in Britain, you probably obtained leave to remain for six months. If you wish to extend your leave to remain in Britain, you must apply for a **residence permit**. In order to obtain a residence permit you must provide evidence that you can financially support yourself and any dependants you have. If it is known that you have claimed any state benefits then you may be refused a residence permit.

The length of the residence permit you are given depends on the length of your course, but will normally be for between three and five years.

What happens if your application is refused?

If the authorities refuse your application for an extension of your leave to remain, they will return your passport and documents to you with a letter stating that your application has been refused and explaining why. The letter will also state whether or not you can

Sample refusal letters

1. *Letter of refusal, giving you the right to appeal against the refusal*

IMMIGRATION ACT 1971

Refusal to revoke or vary leave to enter or remain

To (name)

You have applied for leave to remain in the United Kingdom as a student at (name of college) but you failed to (reasons given for refusal).

The Secretary of State therefore refuses your application. Under the Immigration (Variation of leave) Order 1976, your stay has been extended to (date). If you do not wish to appeal, you should leave the United Kingdom by that date.

You are entitled to appeal against this decision under section 14(1) of the Immigration Act 1971 to the independent appellate authorities established under that act. If you wish to appeal you should complete the attached form and return it to the Under Secretary of State, Home Office (Appeals Section), Lunar House, Wellesley Road, Croydon CR9 2BY, to arrive not later than 14 days after the date of this notice. The Home Office will transmit your notice of appeal to the appellate authorities.

The United Kingdom Immigrants Advisory Service, a voluntary organisation independent of the Government, will advise you, if you wish, about the decision which has been taken against you and on whether to exercise your right of appeal. If you decide to appeal, the service can also help you to prepare your appeal and to present it to the appellate authorities. These services are provided free of charge. The London office of the service is at 190 Great Dover Street, London SE1 (telephone 01 357 6917). The service has other offices at Birmingham, Folkestone, Leeds, Manchester, Southampton, Heathrow Airport, Gatwick Airport and Glasgow.

Signed:

On behalf of the Secretary of State

Date:

---

2. *Letter of refusal, with no right of appeal*

IMMIGRATION ACT 1971

Refusal to grant leave to remain or to vary leave to enter

To (name)

You have applied for leave to remain in the United Kingdom as a student at (name of college) but you failed to (reasons for refusal).

The Secretary of State therefore refuses your application.

Under section 14(1) of the Immigration Act 1971 an entitlement to appeal against a refusal to vary a limited leave is conferred only on a person whose limited leave to enter or remain has not expired.

Your application was received on (date) but your limited leave expired on (earlier date). You therefore have no right of appeal against the Secretary of State's decision.

I have to remind you that because of your limited leave to enter or remain has expired you should leave the United Kingdom without delay. If you fail to leave you may be prosecuted for an offence under the Immigration Act, the penalty for which is a fine of up to £200 and up to six months' imprisonment, and you will also be liable to deportation.

Signed:

On behalf of the Secretary of State

Date:

---

appeal against this decision if you feel that the reasons given for the refusal are unjustified. If you have been given the chance to appeal, you will be sent a form (**APP 1**) to fill in to notify the Home Office that you intend to appeal.

REASONS FOR A REFUSAL

There are a number of **grounds** (reasons) the Home Office can give for refusing your application for an extension of leave to remain. In their letter of refusal, the Home Office can state any one, or several, of these reasons, which are listed on pages 94 and 95.

Extending your leave to remain

Applications in writing

1. Send documents listed below to The Home Office in Croydon. If you are in Northern Ireland send them to the office in Belfast (addresses in Appendix 3).
2. Send documents by *recorded delivery*.
3. Make sure you keep the receipt given to you at the post office. This provides you with proof that you sent the documents and proof of the date you sent them.
4. Keep a photocopy of everything you send to the Home Office.

Advantages

● People who expect to have some problems with their application should apply in writing.

Disadvantages

● Written applications take quite a long time to process, at least a month. You will not have the use of your passport during this time (this is an important consideration if you are planning a holiday or a trip overseas).

Applications in person

1. Take the documents listed below to either: The Home Office, in Croydon; or a local Immigration Office. Local Immigration Offices can be found in Belfast, Glasgow, Harwich, Liverpool, Norwich and Southampton (addresses in Appendix 3).

Advantages

● Personal applications are quicker.
● You do not lose the use of your passport for several weeks.

Disadvantages

● You may have to wait around at the Immigration Office for a full day before you are dealt with, especially if you go to the main office in Croydon. Take a book to read!

Documents required

● Your **passport.**
● Your **police registration certificate** (if you have one).
● A **letter from your college** confirming that you are continuing in full-time study (fifteen hours per week), or that you are beginning a new course.
● **Proof** that you have **enough money** to cover your fees and living expenses for the following year (a bank statement or evidence that you are receiving a scholarship).
● (For written applications only) completed form RON 52(S) **Application to stay in the United Kingdom as a student,** which can be obtained from a Citizens Advice Bureau, from your college welfare officer or from an Immigration Office. If you cannot obtain this form, you can, instead, enclose a letter from yourself which requests an extension of your leave to remain and lists the documents you are enclosing.

Reasons for a refusal	Action to take	How to avoid this
You are not enrolled on a full-time course. If you were between courses or near the end of a course when you applied, you would not have been able to produce evidence that you were enrolled at college.	Enrol on a course as soon as possible.	Organise your course arrangements before you apply to the Home Office. If you have a provisional place at a college, which depends on exam results, ask the college to write a letter explaining this.
You have not got enough money to pay your fees or support yourself. If the Home Office do not see evidence of sufficient money in your bank account, or of money paid in regularly, or if you still owe the college fees, they will refuse you.	If you are on a scholarship, get a letter from your sponsor which says that your money is guaranteed. If not, provide a letter from your bank, or some other form of evidence, saying that you do have the money.	Make sure you have enough money, and the evidence, before you apply to the Home Office. If you do not have enough money in your bank for a good reason — ie foreign exchange problems – include a letter with your evidence explaining this.
Your attendance at college has been poor. Sometimes the Home Office contacts colleges. Have you attended lectures and tutorials regularly? If you have been absent, did you have a good reason?	Explain your absences if necessary. A letter from a doctor or a hospital would be good evidence of genuine illness.	If you need to be absent from college, tell them when and why you will be away.
You are taking a series of unrelated courses. The Home Office will think that you are using student status as an excuse to stay in Britain — especially if you do a course in accounting, another in music, and then a third in furniture making, for example.	Explain why you have chosen your course(s). You should have a logical plan to your studies. If you are studying for a professional qualification get a letter from the professional institution involved explaining the details of the course you are taking.	Try not to change course unless absolutley necessary. If you do more than one course, try to make sure that the second one is of a higher standard than the first — this will appear more logical to the Home Office.

Reasons for a refusal	Action to take	How to avoid this
You have persistently failed your examinations. If this has happened several times before, the Home Office will think that you are not a serious student.	If possible, get a letter explaining why you have failed your exams. For example, if the college put you in a class which was too dificult for you, or if several other students in the class had similar problems. Get a reference from the college saying that you are a genuine student.	Don't apply for courses which might be too difficult or for which you don't have the necessary qualifications.
Your first course was financed by a scholarship, and now you are applying for another course. The Home Office will probably refuse you.		If you wish to stay in Britain to take another course, you need a letter of permission from your original sponsor, even if this sponsor is not financing your next course.
The Home Office thinks you want to remain in Britain permanently. The Home Office might have a number of reasons for thinking this, for example, if you have made enquiries about working in Britain, or about permanent residence in Britain, or if you have told a Home Office official you would like to live in Britain.	It is difficult to prove that you do not intend to live in Britain. Do you have evidence to show that you are going to return to your home country — for example, evidence of a job waiting for you when you return?	Be careful what you say to Home Officials. If they ask you if you want to stay in Britain, say no. If you make any enquiries about permanent residence, do so anonymously.
You have claimed Housing Benefit, Family Credit or Income Support (except the emergency support under regulation 70(3)a).		Do not claim these benefits.
The Home Office thinks you are 'not a genuine student'. This reason is usually given with one of the above reasons.	This is very difficult to disprove.	

HOW TO MAKE AN APPEAL

If the Home Office gives you the right to appeal against its decision *use this right* and make an appeal. *Do not* make your appeal without first getting help and advice from either:

- your college welfare office;
- your college student union;
- one of the organisations listed in Appendix 2.

Other points to remember when making an appeal

- You must complete and return the appeal notice form *within fourteen days from the date you were refused* (not fourteen days from the date you received the letter of refusal).

- If you have a *good* reason (for example a postal strike) for missing the fourteen days deadline then the Home Office will give you fourteen more days to return your notice of appeal. Moving house and not informing anyone of your new address is *not* a good enough reason for missing the deadline.

- Keep copies of all correspondence you have with the Home Office. Send correspondence by recorded delivery so that you have proof of the date you posted it. Don't forget to keep the receipt given to you at the post office.

- Once you have returned the notice of appeal, your right to remain in Britain is protected.

- Even if you think that your appeal will be unsuccessful, you should still make an appeal. The process usually takes quite a long time, sometimes up to twelve months, and this may give you the extra time you need to complete your course or to finish your examinations.

After you have returned your notice of appeal, you will receive a letter informing you when your case is being heard by an adjudicator. You will be asked whether or not you wish to be present at the hearing. If you decide to go to the hearing it is important to have someone to go with you. This should be the person who helped you to make your appeal.

What to do if you have no right of appeal

If you have not been given the right of appeal, but you think that the decision of the Home Office was the result of a mistake or of a misunderstanding, go to your college welfare office, student union or one of the organisations listed in Appendix 2, and explain what has happened. They will look at the details of your case and if they agree that the refusal of your application was unjustified, they will make what is called a **special representation** to the Home Office.

It's not a good idea to ask a solicitor to help you to make an appeal or to make a special representation. The services of organisations such as **UKCOSA, UKIAS** or the **National Union of Students** are free of charge. They also specialise in dealing with such matters, whereas a solicitor may not be a specialist in immigration law. If your appeal and any special representations are unsuccessful, then the Home Office will ask you to leave the country. If you do not leave the country, you will be committing a criminal offence and could be deported.

CHANGING IMMIGRATION STATUS

While you are in Britain as a student, you may have reason to change your immigration status. This means that being a student is not your *main* reason for remaining in Britain. Students can apply to change their immigration status in any of the following circumstances:

● getting married;
● seeking political asylum;
● applying for permanent resident (EC nationals only).

If you think that you are entitled to apply for a change in your immigration status for any other reason not mentioned above, contact one of the organisations listed in Appendix 2 *before* contacting the Home Office.

Marriage to a British citizen
If, while you are a student, you marry a person who has permanent residence in Britain and who lives in Britain, you too can *eventually* obtain permanent residence. After the marriage has taken place, you should take the steps listed on page 98.

Fiancées
Perhaps you are planning to get married, but not immediately. At the same time, you may be aware that your leave to remain as a student will have expired before the date of the marriage. To avoid rushing into a marriage, you can, *but only if you are a female student*, apply to remain in Britain as a fiancée for a period of three months.

Action to take

1. Write to the Home Office enclosing:

   your passport;

   your partner's passport or birth certificate;

   the marriage certificate;

   a letter from yourself requesting leave to remain as the husband/wife of a British citizen or of someone with permanent residence.

2. While the Home Office is considering your application, you may be asked for further information to support your case. You and your partner may be asked to attend an interview. The Home Office has to be satisfied that:

   you are not getting married only for the purpose of remaining in Britain;

   you and your wife/husband have adequate accommodation;

   between you, you have enough money to support yourselves without claiming state benefits;

   you have not previously broken the immigration regulations;

   you are not about to be deported for any reason.

3. If your application is successful, you will be given leave to remain, as the husband/wife of a British citizen, for one year. During that year you should consider the following points:

   Your immigration status is no longer that of a student and therefore you may work, without applying for a work permit.

   You will be eligible to apply for state benefits, but don't, if at all possible. If you do, it may affect your chances of being given permanent residence.

   If you are planning to begin a new course of study during this year, don't. You will still be charged the higher fees paid by students from overseas. Wait until you have been given permanent residence.

4. After that year, you are eligible to apply for **permanent residence** or **settled status.** The two terms mean the same thing.

5. The Home Office will grant you permanent residence if you still satisfy the conditions listed in 2, above.

6. Once you have permanent residence, you have the following rights:

   you can stay permanently in Britain;

   you are free to leave and enter Britain at any time, on the condition that you don't stay out of Britain for more than two years;

   you become eligible to pay the lower, home student, rate of fees for any new course you begin (but not for any course you had already started before you were given permanent residence);

   after three years, you can apply for British nationality. This will cost you a fee of £60.

Points to note

Make sure that your own leave to remain as a student has not expired before you get married, otherwise you will lose your right of appeal if your application is refused.

If the marriage takes place only a few days before your present leave to remain is due to expire, the Home Office may suspect that the marriage is not genuine, but has taken place so that one of you can remain in Britain.

If your application is refused, you can appeal against the decision.

Marriage to another student from overseas

If you are a *female* student and want to marry someone who is in Britain as a student, you can *either*:

- leave your own student status unchanged; *or*
- apply to remain in Britain as the wife of a student from overseas.

The second option would be the best if your own leave to remain as a student is due to expire before that of your husband. If you are given leave to remain as the wife of a student from overseas, you can then work or study part time. But *don't forget* that as soon as your husband's leave to remain as a student expires, your right to remain also expires with it.

Political asylum

If, while you are in Britain, political events in your home country make you afraid to return there, because of your race, nationality, political opinion or religion, you can apply for **asylum** in Britain.

This type of application is not easy to make, and you *must* obtain advice from one of the organisations which specialise in helping people to seek asylum. You can find their addresses and telephone numbers in Appendix 2.

- The British Refugee Council
- The United Kingdom Immigration Advisory Service (Refugee Unit)
- United Kingdom Council For Overseas Student Affairs

Permanent residence (EC nationals only)

This *only* applies to EC nationals who have been *working* in Britain for a period of four years continuously. If you have a residence permit for five years, and for the last four of those years you have been in employment or self-employed, you can apply for permanent residence. If you have remained in Britain for four years as a *student*, you are *not* entitled to apply for permanent residence.

TRAVELLING ABROAD

If you are planning to leave Britain for a short time, to take a holiday or to make a short visit home, make sure that you have all the required documentation before you leave. Take the following steps at least three months, if possible, before you are going to leave Britain.

1. Check what documents you need to enter the countries you are going to visit or travel through (eg visa).

2.   Check that your passport will not expire while you are away. If so, apply for a new one immediately. Do not leave Britain without a valid passport.

3.   Check that your current leave to remain in Britain will not expire before you return to Britain. If it is due to expire, you must apply to the Home Office for an extension of your stay *before you leave Britain*. It is better to make the application in person rather than by post, as postal applications can take some time to be processed and the Home Office might not have returned your passport when you want to travel. You will not be able to obtain a re-entry visa (see point 4) if your current leave to remain is due to expire, or will expire while you are out of Britain.

4.   Check whether you need a *re-entry visa*. If you are a *visa national* (see page 79), and needed a visa to enter Britain, then you will need a re-entry visa. You can obtain a re-entry visa from one of the local passport offices listed below. You can apply in person or by post. The cost of a re-entry visa is currently £20.

London

Passport Office
Clive House
70 Petty France
London SW1H 9HD
Tel: (01) 271 8560

Glasgow

Passport Office
3 Northgate
96 Milton Street
Cowcaddens
Glasgow
Tel: (041) 332 0271

Liverpool

Passport Office
5th Floor
India Buildings
Water Street
Liverpool L2 0QZ
Tel: (051) 237 3010

Newport

Passport Office
Olympia House
Upper Dock Street
Newport
Gwent, Wales
Tel: (0633) 56292

Peterborough

Passport Office
55 Westfield Road
Peterborough
PE3 6TG
Tel: (0722) 895 555

Belfast

Passport Office
47-53 High Street
Belfast BT1 2QS
Tel: (0232) 232 371

All local passport offices are open from 9.00am to 4.30pm, Monday to Friday.

5.   *Whenever* you leave Britain, even if only for one day, *always*

carry with you **evidence** that you are a student and that you have enough money to support yourself while in Britain.

Emergencies

If you need to travel in a hurry, and don't have time to extend your leave to remain or obtain a re-entry visa before you leave, you can:

- obtain an extension of your stay as you re-enter Britain. In order to do this you will need the same documents and evidence listed on page 93.

- obtain a re-entry visa from the British Embassy or High Commission in the country you are visiting. You will need all the documentation listed on page 76. This should *only* be done in an emergency. It is much easier to obtain a re-entry visa in Britain. Problems, such as not having the correct documentation, are easier to solve if you are in Britain. If you have to wait for documents or letters to be sent from Britain, you might be delayed abroad for some time.

5
Accommodation

Before you leave your home country, make sure that you have arranged for somewhere to live in Britain, even if it is only temporary accommodation.

Do not come to Britain hoping that you will be able to find accommodation when you arrive. Accommodation is not easy to find, especially in September when thousands of other new students are also looking for somewhere to live. It can take weeks to find suitable accommodation, or accommodation that you can afford.

As a student, there will be a variety of different types of accommodation available to you. The types of accommodation can be divided into two main categories:

- Accommodation owned and maintained by the college where you will be studying. Universities and polytechnics are more likely to have this type of accommodation than smaller colleges.

- Private accommodation, unconnected with the college but which the college *may* find for you, or help you to find.

If you are coming to Britain for the first time, it is probably a good idea to use the college accommodation. It is difficult to organise private accommodation if you aren't in Britain. Also, college accommodation provides a comfortable base from which you can get to know the town or city where you are studying and discover the type of accommodation you might want to move to later on.

Most colleges which have their own accommodation give priority to new students. Some colleges will guarantee accommodation to students from overseas for the duration of their course.

As soon as you know that you have a place at a college:

1. Find out whether the college provides accommodation.

2. If the college does provide accommodation, they will ask you to complete a form requesting accommodation. They will normally send this form to you along with the offer of a place on a course. There will be a closing date for applications for accommodation, so return the form before this date.

3. If the college does not provide accommodation find out whether there is an **accommodation office,** or someone at the college who helps students to find accommodation.

4. If not, you must begin to look for your own accommodation.

TYPES OF ACCOMMODATION YOU CAN ARRANGE BEFORE TRAVELLING TO BRITAIN

Accommodation provided by the college	*Private accommodation*
Halls of residence	Hostels
Self-catering halls of residence	Lodgings
Self-catering college houses or flats	Temporary accommodation (hotels, guest houses, transit accommodation)

● **Halls of residence** — These are large buildings which provide accommodation for large numbers of students in either single or shared rooms (maximum of two people in a room). Some halls accommodate male students or female students only. Others take both male and female students and these are usually called **mixed** halls. Most halls of residence provide three meals per day. Some provide only breakfast and an evening meal, with lunch provided at weekends.

● **Self-catering halls of residence** — These are like halls of residence in every way except that residents buy and prepare their own food. Bedrooms are usually arranged in small groups around a kitchen which you share with other students.

● **Self-catering college houses or flats** — These are flats or houses which are owned and maintained by the college. Again, students must buy and prepare their own food. Some colleges allocate a few of these houses or flats for students with families, but there is always a shortage of this type of accommodation.

● **Hostels** — The best alternative to college accommodation is a hostel, especially if this is your first time in Britain. Hostels are very similar to college halls of residence. They usually provide meals, although a small number are self-catering. You will probably find many other students from different colleges also living in the hostel, so you probably won't be lonely. Many hostels have long waiting lists, so apply for a place in a hostel well in advance. Lists of hostels can be obtained from:

Your local British Council office,

The London Tourist Board,

The Young Women's Christian Association of Great Britain (YWCA),

The National Council of Young Men's Christian Associations (YMCA),

International Students' House (ISH).

See Appendix 6 for addresses.

- **Lodgings** — If you are living in lodgings, sometimes referred to as **digs,** it means that you are renting a room in someone's home. It may be the home of a family with children, a couple or a single person. Being in lodgings can be like living at home, but with a different family and you may have to change your lifestyle to fit in with theirs. You may not have as much freedom as you would like, but having this type of accommodation does mean that you will have plenty of company.

  The accommodation office at the college where you are going to study will probably have lists of local families who take lodgers. If you are going to live in London, there is an organisation called The **Student Accommodation Service** which arranges accommodation with British families. Their address is 67 Wigmore Street, London W1H 9LG. Tel (01) 935 9979.

- **Temporary accommodation** — Even if you have not arranged your long-term accommodation, you must arrange some temporary accommodation before you leave. It may not be ideal accommodation, it will probably be quite expensive, but it will be a base from which you can search for something more permanent. It is obviously easier to look around for somewhere to live, once you are in Britain. When you are organising temporary accommodation, arrange to stay there for several weeks, rather than just a few days. It may take some time to find the accommodation you really want. Also, you might want to settle into your new college and your course before moving home again. The beginning of a new term at college is always very hectic. If you spend all your time looking for accommodation you may miss some of the events which have been arranged for new students.

Alternatively, you could come to Britain several weeks before your course begins, so that you have plenty of spare time to find accommodation. Temporary accommodation can be arranged through:

The London Tourist Board,
The British Tourist Authority,
The YMCA and YWCA (both these organisations have hostels throughout Britain, some of which provide temporary accommodation. People of any religion are accepted),
The Youth Hostels Association.

See Appendix 6 for addresses.

● **Transit accommodation** — If you have to travel through London on your way to another part of Britain, you may require overnight accommodation. The British Council can organise this for you. Write to The Arrivals Group, 10 Spring Gardens, London SW1A 2BN, *one month before you wish to travel,* telling them the date, place and time you are due to arrive and your flight number. They will arrange for someone to meet you at their office in Victoria Station and to take you to a hotel. The London Tourist Board can also arrange transit accommodation. You should expect to pay between £12 and £30 per night, but check the price before accepting the booking.

● **Married students and families** — It is much more difficult for a married couple to find student accommodation, especially if they have children. Only a few colleges have accommodation especially for families, but this is very limited. If you are planning to bring your wife/husband and children, it's good idea to travel to Britain several weeks *in advance* of the beginning of your course. Come alone first of all. Then, when you have found suitable accommodation, the rest of your family can join you.

CHANGING YOUR ACCOMMODATION

When you have spent some time in Britain, you might want to move out of accommodation provided by the college and into accommodation of your own choice, where you will feel more independent. You may have found a group of friends and decided that you want to share a flat or house with them.

Unfortunately, you may have no choice about moving out as there are a few colleges which can only provide accommodation for students in their first year of studies.

Accommodation which is not provided by the college is usually called **private sector accommodation.** Both types of accommodation have their advantages and disadvantages.

Disadvantages of college accommodation

- You lose some independence. Some halls of residence have rules about the time you have to be in at night, whether you can have guests in your room, and so on.

- It is more difficult to be alone. You have to be strict with people who 'pop in' (visit), uninvited, for a chat when you are trying to study.

- You have to eat your meals at specific times.

- In some halls of residence, you have to move out of your room during the holidays. This can be a problem if you are not intending to go home for the holidays. Many colleges now make sure that students from overseas are put into rooms which will not need to be vacated during the holidays. Ask about this when you apply for your accommodation.

- You can become very sheltered and protected from life outside college. If your hall of residence is on a campus, you can find yourself becoming separated from the outside world. Some people may see this as an advantage.

Disadvantages of private sector accommodation

- Your accommodation could be situated very far from the college.

- You will have to deal with things like gas or electricity bills which are not usually included in the price of the accommodation.

- You have to clean your own room, provide and launder your own bed linen.

- There won't always be someone immediately available to fix things that break down. You may have to cope with things like a leaking roof, blocked drains, faulty heating system.

- There is more chance of becoming lonely.

- It is less secure than college accommodation. You may find yourself being asked to move out half way through a term.

TYPES OF PRIVATE ACCOMMODATION

Bedsits/bedsitters

Old, large houses are often divided up into bedsits, which are then rented out to individuals. The term bedsit usually refers to one room, where you live, eat, sleep and sometimes cook. If the cooking facilities are not in the room, you will probably have to share them with someone else living in the same house or block. You will also have to share the toilet and bathroom with other people. You rent the room from a **landlord** or **landlady**, the owner of the building. Sometimes the landlord will also live in the building.

You will probably have to clean your own rooms and do your own laundry. You will also have to provide your own blankets, sheets and towels. People in bedsits usually pay for their gas and electricity by putting coins into a meter which is inside their room.

Life in a bedsit gives you plenty of freedom, but it can also be very lonely living on your own in one room. The other people in the building may not all be students and may not wish to get to know their neighbours.

Flatshares

This means renting a bedroom in a large flat or house and sharing all the other facilities, for example the living room, kitchen and bathroom, with the other people living in the flat or house.

You may not know the other people living there, so taking the room could be a risk in case you don't get on with them, but it can also be a good way of making new friends.

When someone leaves the flat or house, and a room becomes free, it is usually the job of the other people living there to arrange for someone to rent the spare room. They will advertise the fact that they have a free room (see page 109), and then select several of the applicants to come to see the room and to meet the other occupants. You then have the opportunity to see whether you will get on with them and they will decide whether they like you. It is rather like an interview!

Everyone living in the flat or house shares the rent and the bills for gas and electricity. In some flatshares the food bills and the cooking are also shared, in others, everyone buys their own food and cooks separately. This is something you have to organise between yourselves. The cleaning and the general caretaking of the flat or house is also shared. There can be problems with sharing a flat or house with other people such as:

- someone not doing their share of cleaning, washing up and so on;
- one person continually using up all the communal food and not replacing it;
- someone with a girlfriend/boyfriend who stays at the house

   regularly, but does not contribute towards the bills;
- someone playing loud music or watching television while you are trying to study;
- very large telephone bills and everyone saying that they never use the telephone.

In order to prevent these problems find out before you move in what the arrangments are for paying bills, cleaning, telephone calls and guests, find out what food is **communal** (this means shared between you all, and is usually things like eggs, milk, bread, coffee, tea) and find out if there are any other 'house rules'.

Rented flats/houses
An alternative type of flatshare is when a group of people who already know each other decide to go and look for an empty flat or house to share together. Don't think that because you are all friends, the same sort of problems will not arise. Living together can often put a strain on a friendship!

Again, it is very important to agree how you are going to deal with bills, housework, guests and so on, *before you start living together.* Don't wait for the problems to arise before thinking about them. This type of accommodation is often the cheapest, but unfortunately it is not easy to find large empty flats and houses, especially in London.

Most of the flats and houses available for renting are referred to as **furnished accommodation.** This usually means that the house or flat contains very basic furniture. **Unfurnished** accommodation is almost impossible to find.

Flats, houses and bedsits can vary a great deal in size and quality, Never agree to take a room or flat without going to see it first.

HOW TO FIND ACCOMMODATION

In your search for somewhere to live be prepared for disappointments. You will find that many of the rooms or flats you enquire about have already been taken and the ones which are still available are not what you really wanted.

August and September are the worst times to go looking for accommodation as this is when most other students are trying to find somewhere to live.

Finding accommodation through your college
If your college has an accommodation office, this is the first place to try. They will have lists of local available accommodation and they

may have even inspected it to make sure that it is of a reasonably good standard. The student union at your college may also be able to help you.

College notice boards are usually good for finding flatshares. You will find that other students use these to advertise vacant rooms in their flat or house. You can also use the noticeboards to advertise the fact that you are looking for accommodation.

ACCOMMODATION WANTED

Girl, aged 19, from Hong Kong looking for bedsit or room in flat. Any area considered. I am a second year student in Maths Dept. Hobbies — Badminton, Tennis, Cooking.

Local newspapers

TWO small rooms, £40 each. Share bathroom and large kitchen. Two large rooms, £45 each. Share kitchen and bathroom. Tel: 249 5473. A18.1

Sample newspaper advertisement for rented accommodation available.

There is usually a section in local newspapers for people to advertise bedsits, flats and houses for rent. You *must* make sure that you get the newspaper as soon as it is printed, and have plenty of change ready for making phone calls.

Newspaper advertisements often use a language of their own. You will probably come across some of the following:

c/h	central heating
gch	gas central heating
wc	toilet ('water closet')
1 recep	one reception (living room or lounge)
s/c	self contained

sleep 3	has three beds (this may mean two bedrooms with two people sharing a room)
3 bed house	three bedrooms
ff	fully furnished
pw/pm	per week/per month
all mod cons	all facilities are up to date ('all modern conveniences')

Shop windows
Newsagents, post offices and some other local shops often have noticeboards in their windows which people use to advertise vacant rooms and flats.

Talking to people
Tell all your friends and fellow students that you are looking for somewhere to live. If anyone knows of a room or flat which is soon going to become vacant, you might be able to get it before it is advertised elsewhere.

Accommodation agencies
Accommodation agencies will help you find accommodation, but they will charge you a fee — sometimes as much as three weeks' rent.

● Before you ask an agency to find accommodation for you, *ask about the fee they charge.*

● *Don't* pay any money to an agency if you have not accepted the accommodation they have found for you. It is *unlawful* for an agency to ask for:
  — a deposit
  — a fee for putting your name on their waiting list
  — a fee for giving you addresses of flats or house to look at.

● An agency can only charge a fee once your have *accepted* accommodation which they have found for you.

If an agency asks you to sign any agreement which you don't understand, *don't sign it.* Take a copy to someone at your college and ask them to explain it to you.

A list of reliable accommodation agencies in London can be obtained from *The London Housing Aid Centre* (address in Appendix 6). If you are not in London, your school or college should be able to recommend a good agency.

Going to see a house or flat

In general, the quality of accommodation available for renting, especially at a price students can afford, is poor. Don't expect too much, as you will probably be disappointed! When you go to look at a room or a house or a flat, there are a number of things to look for:

- Are there any signs of **damp** (peeling wallpaper, flaking paint)?

- Does the room feel **warm** or **cold?** Does the sun shine into it? If it is summer, and the room feels cold, imagine how it will feel in winter. Don't forget that you will be paying for your own heating bills.

- Do all the **electrical/gas appliances** work? Test lights, cooker, heaters and so on.

- Make sure **windows** close properly. Make sure that you can open them as well.

THE FORMALITIES OF RENTING ACCOMMODATION

When you rent a bedsit, room, flat or house, you are entering into a legal agreement called a **tenancy agreement.** People under the age of 18 are *not* allowed, by law, to hold tenancy agreements. When renting accommodation:

- Never be satisfied with a verbal agreement. Get everything in writing.
- Do not sign any complicated contracts or agreements which you don't understand.
- Make sure you know exactly what you are agreeing to before you sign anything.
- Make sure you know exactly what is and is not going to be included in your rent (for example, gas, electricity, rates).
- If you don't understand what is written in a contract, take it to someone at your college and ask them to explain it to you.
- Keep a photocopy of everything you have signed.
- Be wary of landlords who try to rush you into signing agreements.
- Make sure that the landlord gives you a **rent book.** This is used to keep a record of all payments you have made.
- If you don't have a rent book, it is wiser to make any payments

by cheque and not by cash. Cheques provide proof of payment.

The various types of **rental agreements** or *tenancies,* you can be offered are described below. Because the tenant law is slightly different in Northern Ireland, students living there should obtain details from **The Northern Ireland Housing Executive,** Advice Centre, 2 May Street, Belfast. Tel: (0232) 240588.

Assured tenancy

This is the best form of rental agreement you can get because it gives you the most security. If you have an assured tenancy:

● the landlord cannot live on the premises;
● a long as you have paid your rent and taken care of the property, you cannot be asked to leave unless by order of a court of law.

Shorthold tennancy

This is a tenancy with a **time limit.** When you begin to live in the accommodation, you have to sign an agreement that you will leave after a fixed time. The length of time specified is decided by the landlord, but it must be longer than six months.

Tenants of resident landlords

This applies if you live in a flat, room or bedsit where the landlord also lives **on the premises,** which means in the same building. This type of tenancy gives you less security than any other.

● The landlord can tell you to leave whenever he wishes.

● If *you* wish to leave, you must give at least four weeks' notice.

● If you share any **facilities** (for example, toilet, kitchen) with the landlord or any member of the landlord's family, you can be forced to leave *without* an order from a court of law.

● If you do not share any facilities, the landlord must obtain a court order before forcing you to leave.

No tenancy agreement at all

Some landlords will not give you any agreement to sign, but will simply take a deposit and give you a key. If this happens, you do have the same legal rights as someone with an assured tenancy. However, it is always better to have everything in writing so *always ask for a tenancy agreement.*

If the landlord refuses to give you an agreement, and if this is the accommodation you really want, then make sure you keep proof of all payments you make to the landlord. If he offers you any of the following types of tenancy agreement:

● Holiday let
● Licence agreement
● Tenancy with board or service

Seek advice from a Citizens Advice Bureau or, if you are in London, an organisation called **SHAC** (see Appendix 6 for address). These types of agreements provide you with very few legal rights as a tenant.

Flatsharers
If several people are sharing a flat or house you may have one of the following arrangements:

● you are **joint** tenants, with *one* tenancy agreement;
● you are **individual** tenants, with *individual* tenancy agreements;
● *one* of you is the tenant, and **sub-lets** to the others.

The situation is quite complicated, so before signing any agreements, get advice from the welfare office at your college or a local Citizens Advice Bureau. *Whichever type of arrangement you finally have, always:*

● have only *one* rent book for the flat/house (not separate books for each person living there);
● pay rent to the landlord in *one* sum, not individually,
● agree with the landlord, that if one person leaves the accommodation, it will be your responsibility (not the landlord's) to replace them.

Leaving your accommodation
When you wish to leave your accommodation, you must give at least one months' notice, in writing (keep a copy), and at the same time pay your rent up until the date you intend to leave.

If you are in a flatshare, and therefore sharing the tenancy of the property with other people, you must also inform them of your intention to leave, as they will have to find someone else to replace you and pay your share of the rent.

Inventories
When you agree to rent a furnished room, house or flat, you will

Sample letter of notice

Dear Mr Gray (landlord's name),

I, Maria Benedetti, hereby give notice of my intention to leave
18 Primrose Street, Hull HU14 7XK, on July 23rd 1989.

I have enclosed my rent up until this date.

Yours sincerely,

Maria Benedetti

Witnessed by (signature of witness) on (date)

probably be given and asked to sign a list of all the furniture and
any other items which are inside it. This list is called an **inventory**.
Before you sign the inventory, check to make sure that everything on
the list really is there and is in working order. If anything is damaged
or broken, make a note of it.

When you leave the accommodation, the inventory will be checked
and you will be asked to pay for anything which is missing or
damaged.

Deposits

When you agree to rent accommodation, you will probably be asked
to pay a **deposit**, which is a sum of money paid to the landlord and
refunded to you when you leave. Deposits are a form of security for
the landlord, in case:

- you don't pay your rent;
- you don't pay your gas/electricity/phone bills;
- you damage the property or any of the contents.

If any of these things happen, your deposit will *not* be refunded to
you.

Different landlords ask for different amounts of money as a
deposit. However, by law, the amount must be *no more than the
equivalent of two months' rent*.

When you pay your deposit, make sure that you:

- get a **receipt**;
- get a **written statement** showing what the deposit covers, and under what circumstances the deposit can be kept by the landlord.

At the same time that you give in your notice of leaving the accommodation, *write* to your landlord and request him/her to come to inspect the property. Keep a copy of this letter. If there is anything which the landlord is not satisfied with, you have time to put it right *before* you leave, and therefore there will be no reason for the landlord to deduct anything from your deposit.

If you do have any problems getting your deposit back, contact your college welfare office or a local Citizens Advice Bureau.

Gas, electricity and telephones

Before you move into new accommodation, you must make sure that the gas board, the electricity board and British Telecom (BT) have read the meters and put everything in your name otherwise you could find yourself paying the bills of the previous tenant!

Decoration and repairs

Make sure that you have a written agreement with the landlord about who is responsible for repairs and general maintenance of the accommodation. Usually, major repairs are the responsibility of the landlord, but it is *your* responsibility to inform him/her as soon as something needs to be repaired.

Landlords usually allow you to make some small changes to the decoration of a room — for example, changing the colour of paint — but don't do anything without asking for permission first!

Some landlords will offer to pay for paint or other materials you use. If so, make sure you are clear about what she/he means. There is no point in buying the most expensive paint you can find when the landlord meant cheap white paint.

Problems with landlords

The law relating to landlords and tenants is quite complicated. If you do have any problems at all with your landlord, seek advice from the welfare officer or student union at your college or from a local Citizens Advice Bureau. If you are in London you can contact an organisation called **SHAC** (address in Appendix 6).

Finally, if you change your accommodation, and you have a police registration card, don't forget to inform the local police station of your new address.

6
Life
in Britain

When you make your travel arrangements, try to make sure that you will arrive in Britain on a **week-day** (Monday, Tuesday, Wednesday, Thursday, Friday), and *not* during the **weekend** (Saturday, Sunday) or on a **public holiday** (see page 128). Most shops and offices are closed at weekends and on public holidays, and trains and buses are less frequent on a Sunday. Try to arrive, if possible, during **office opening hours** (9.00 a.m — 5.00 p.m) just in case you have any problems which need to be sorted out. The best time to arrive in Britain is in the morning. This gives your plenty of time to reach your final destination. If your final destination is not London, it might be cheaper for you to book a flight to the British airport nearest to your destination.

FIRST STEPS ON BRITISH SOIL

When you have been through passport control, you will be able to collect your luggage (unless you have travelled by sea and already have your luggage with you) and go through customs.

Luggage retrieval and customs

Before you collect your lugguage, try to find a luggage trolley with wheels, to put luggage on. Some of the airports in Britain are very large, especially Heathrow, and you will have to walk a long way before you reach the exit.

You will probably find that all the luggage from your flight is on a large circular conveyor belt. When you see your luggage go past, take it off the moving belt, but don't worry if you miss it because it will come round again. Don't panic if you can only see one of your suitcases. They very rarely come off the plane all together and you may have to wait for a while before you see the rest of your luggage.

When you have collected all your luggage, go through **customs**.

Customs

At customs you will find more queues. You will have a choice of two ways to go through:

the green channel — which means you have *nothing to declare;*
the red channel — which means you have *goods to declare.*

If you are carrying more than your allowance of duty and tax free goods, or any prohibited goods, you must pass through the *red* channel.

If you go through the *green* channel the customs officer may still stop you and ask you open your luggage. This does not mean that he suspects you of smuggling goods into Britain. Customs officers are required to make random checks on all passengers.

The current allowance is shown in the chart on page 118. You are entitled to the allowance in *either* column one *or* column two, but not both.

For further details about what can and cannot be brought into Britain, contact your local British Embassy.

People under the age of 17 are not entitled to tobacco and drinks allowances.

You may have to wait awhile before all of your luggage
appears at the airport.

The Current Customs Allowance
COLUMN 1   *or*   COLUMN 2

Goods obtained duty or tax free in the EC, or duty and tax free on a ship or aircraft, or goods obtained outside the EC.

Goods obtained duty and tax paid in The EC.

Tobacco products
(double if you live outside Europe)

Tobacco products

200 cigarettes
or
100 cigarillos
or
50 cigars
or
250 grams of tobacco

300 cigarettes
or
150 cigarillos
or
75 cigars
or
400 grams of tobacco

Alcoholic drinks

2 litres of still table wine
plus
1 litre over 22% vol, (eg spirits)
or
2 litres not over 22% vol, (eg low strength liqueurs, sparkling wines, fortified wines)
or
A further 2 litres of still table wine

Alcholic drinks

5 litres of still table wine
plus
1 1/2 litres over 22% vol.
or
3 litres not over 22% vol.

or
A further 3 litres of still table wine

Perfume

50 grams

Perfume

75 grams

Toilet water

250cc

Toilet water

375cc

Other goods

£28 worth, but no more than 50 litres of beer
25 mechanical lighters

Other goods

£207 worth, but no more than 50 litres of beer
25 mechanical lighters

- *Prohibited goods* are; counterfeit coins; drugs, including opium, heroine, amphetamines, morphine, cocaine, LSD; firearms and ammunition; explosives; flick knives; horror comics; obscene books, magazines and films; radio transmitters; most animals and birds (dead or alive), meat or poultry; plants, bulbs, trees and certain vegetables and fruits.

- *Prescribed drugs.* If you are carrying any drugs which have been prescribed by a doctor, you must produce evidence of this. Get a letter from your doctor before leaving your home country.

- *Pets.* You cannot bring any animals into Britain without a permit. If you wish to bring an animal, it must go into quarantine for a period of six months.

Left luggage

If you have just arrived in a city and need to look for a hotel, or if you are passing through, and want to spend a few hours looking around, You can usually leave luggage at an airport or a large railway station by using:

- *Left luggage lockers.* These cost between £1.50 and £4, depending on the size you choose. They look like lots of metal cupboards in rows. You have to insert money into a slot to release the key. Put your luggage inside, lock the door and don't forget to take the key with you!
- *Left luggage office.* To leave your luggage at the left luggage office costs between £2.50 and £3. Don't forget to find out when the office closes and reopens. It is not usual to find these offices open all night. When you leave your luggage you will be given a ticket which you will need when you want to collect it.

Not all stations have both types of luggage facility. Smaller stations will not have either.

REGISTERING WITH THE POLICE

If you are required to register with the police, you must do this within seven days of arrival in Britain.

The stamp which the Immigration Officer put into your passport when you arrived will tell you if you need to register with the police. You do not normally have to register with the police if you are:

- a student who is visiting Britain for less than six months;
- a student from an EC country;

- a student from a commonwealth country.

To register, go to the police station nearest to where you are living. You may be able to register there, or they will tell you where you must go to register. If you are living in London, register at **The Aliens's Registration Office**, 10 Lambs Conduit Street, London WC1N 3NX (open Monday to Friday, 9.00 a.m — 4.45 p.m).

To register you will need:

- your passport,
- two small photographs or yourself,
- £25 per person *over* the age of 16.

Each time you change your accommodation, and each time you extend your leave to remain, you *must* register again. You do not, however, need to pay the fee again, unless you lose your registration document.

TELEPHONES

You will find **public telephones** at all airports, seaports railway stations, bus stations, some post offices and in the streets.

Unfortunately, the familiar large red telephone boxes are disappearing and are being replaced by more modern **booths**. Clear instructions on how to use the telephone are printed inside the phone booths.

Most modern telephones will accept any kind of coin. A small screen shows you how much money you have put in, how much you have left and when you need to insert more money during your call. Older phones will only accept 10p coins. When the 10p has finished you will hear a rapid *pip, pip, pip* noise which means you should insert more coins.

Some telephones do *not* take coins but are operated by a small green plastic card called a **phone card**. If it is a phone card telephone, you will see the green phone card symbol. You can buy phone cards from post offices and shops which also display this symbol.

The cost of a phone call depends on the time of day you are making your call. Calls are cheapest between **6 p.m and 8 a.m,** Monday to Friday, and all day on Saturday and Sunday. The most expensive time to make a call is between 9 a.m and 1 p.m Monday to Friday.

If your call is a local one, made after 6 p.m, **10p** will last for over five minutes. A long distance call (within Britain) made after 6 p.m, will cost between 15p and 35p for five minutes.

When you pick up the phone and have inserted your money, you

will hear a low purring noise. This is the **dialling tone,** and it means
that the phone is ready for you to dial the number. If you are making
the call to a phone in Britain, when you have dialled the number you
will hear one of the following noises:

- *Ring, ring, pause — ring, ring, pause.* This means that the phone
  at the other end is ringing.
- *Pip, pip, pip, pip (continuous).* This means that the phone at the
  other end is occupied. This is called the **engaged tone.**
- *One continuous note.* This means that the phone at the other end
  is out of order, or that the number you have dialled does not
  exist.

Telephone numbers
In Britain, telephone numbers are written as *groups* of numbers. For
example:

(01) 580 9754

(0223) 654769

The first number, in brackets, is the code number for the town you
are dialling. For example:

01 is the code for London

0223 is the code for Cambridge.

Therefore, if you are dialling *from* London you omit the 01 part of
the number. If you are dialling *from* Cambridge, you omit the 0223
part of the number.

In order to make a call overseas, add **010** to the beginning of the
number, followed by the **country code** and then the rest of the
number.

If you have any problems with a phone, dial **100** which will connect
you, free of charge, to the **operator** who will help you to make your
call.

If you want to phone someone in Britain, but you don't have their
telephone number, you can ring **directory enquiries,** free of charge,
by dialling **192.** They will ask you for the name of the town, the name
of the person you want to phone and the name of the street or area
they live in.

THE POST OFFICE

If you wish to send anything by post, you can buy stamps at a **post
office** and some newsagents.

Post offices are usually open from 9.00 a.m to 5.30 p.m Monday to

Friday, and on Saturday mornings. Some of them also have machines in the wall outside, so that you can buy stamps when the post office is closed.

If you have a parcel or a heavy letter, go inside to have it weighed so you can put the correct amount of stamps on it. If you are sending a parcel overseas, you will also have to complete a customs form.

You can send letters and parcels by **first class** or by **second class** post. First class letters posted to an address within Britain will probably arrive the following day. Second class post is cheaper but takes longer, about two to three days. British post boxes are always red.

Current postal rates are shown in this table.

	Letters within Britain		Letters to Europe (airmail)
	1st class	2nd class	
under 20 grams	20p	15p	24p
20g — 60g	20p	15p	41p
60g — 100g	28p	24p	44p
100g — 150g	34p	28p	60p
150g — 200g	42p	34p	80p
Airmail letter to ALL other countries:- Under 10g — 30—35p each additional 10g — an extra 12—16p			

Important deliveries

If you are sending anything important or valuable through the post, send it by **Recorded Delivery** or by **Registered Post.**

Recorded delivery provides the sender with proof of postage and proof that the letter has been received. It costs an extra 25p.

Registering a letter provides proof of postage, proof of delivery, special security handling and compensation if the item is lost. This costs between £1.59 and £1.89. Never send cash through the post. Money should be sent by using **Postal Orders** or **International Money Orders,** which can be bought at the post office.

SHOPPING AND CONSUMER RIGHTS

In the past, shopping was done in the local **high street,** where you could find every shop you might need. Although you will still find high streets in smaller towns, most towns now have at least one **supermarket,** which is a large store selling all types of foods and many household items. You will also find **corner shops** selling food and household items near to your house or flat. Although supermarkets are cheaper, local shops are usually more convenient if you only need to buy one or two items.

In larger towns you will find that the high street has been taken over by clothes shops, shoe shops, television and video shops, chemists, and so on. In some towns, you will find all these shops in a covered area — a **shopping centre.**

Another type of all-in-one shop is the **department store,** which you can find in most large towns and cities. This is a large shop, several floors (storeys) high, which sells clothes, household items, furniture, electrical goods, and, in some cases, food as well — in fact, almost everything. Each floor is usually dedicated to a particular type of item. Department stores often have restaurants or coffee bars inside them, and sometimes telephones and public toilets.

A good place to find bargains is at the local **outdoor market.** Some towns have a market open every day. Others have a market only one day a week. Even if you don't want to buy anything, a market is an interesting place to visit and can be a good source of free entertainment.

At some markets you will only find food, but larger markets have stalls selling cheap clothes and many other items. Some items on market stalls are cheap because they are **seconds** — items of inferior quality. Many items are of perfect quality but are cheap simply because they have come directly from the factory, or because a stall-holder doesn't have to pay the high price of owning or renting a shop.

Bargains in things like fruit and vegetables can be found if you go to a market at the end of the day. Stall-holders will be eager to sell everything before they pack up to go home, and so will reduce the price.

Useful facts about shopping in Britain

● Shopping hours are usually between 9.00am and 5.30pm Monday to Saturday. Some shops, especially local ones, open later in the evening and also on Sundays.

● All prices are fixed by the shop owner. **Bartering,** trying to get a lower price, does not happen in Britain, even in markets.

● The price of an item often depends on the shop. If you are going to buy something expensive, always check the price in several different shops before buying.

- In supermarkets, you take a wire basket or trolley to collect your items as you go round the store. You then pay for everything at the **check-out.**Be careful not to put any items in your own bag by mistake.

- In a department store, you must pay for each item at the nearest desk — you cannot carry items around from floor to floor.

- Most supermarkets do not provide free bags to carry away your shopping. You have to pay for them.

- Don't wait for someone to pack your shopping for you. You have to do it yourself.

- If you see a shop displaying the word SALE in the window, it means that they are selling items at reduced prices.

Consumer rights

If you find that something you have bought is faulty, damaged or does not work, you can take it back to the shop and get a replacement or your money back. In order to do this you must have the **receipt,** the piece of paper which was given to you when you paid for the item.

If you find you are having a problem with a shop, go to your local Citizens Advice Bureau.

ELECTRICAL ITEMS

If you bring any electrical items, remember that the voltage in Britain is **AC 240V.**

It might be easier to buy what you need when you get to Britain, or to bring battery operated items. *Electrical items sold in Britain do not have plugs fitted to them.* You will have to do that yourself. You will also probably have to change the fuse in the plug. Most plugs will be already fitted with a **13 amp fuse** but you may have to change it to a 5 amp or a 3 amp one. The box containing the electrical item should tell you which size fuse you need.

If you haven't fitted a plug before, ask someone to do if for you.

LIBRARIES

No one expects you to buy all the books on a college reading list, even if you can afford to. You should therefore join a **library.**

If your school or college does not have a library of its own, you might want to join your local public library. Local libraries, as well as being places where you can sit and read or study in peace and comfort, allow members to borrow books to take home. They are also useful centres of local information on things like welfare services in your area, social events, and places of interest.

Your local library may not have all the books you require, but once you are a member, you can ask your library to order books you need from another library in Britain. Joining a library is free. All you have to do is fill in a form at the library and provide proof of your address.

TV LICENCES

If you do not live in college accommodation, and you wish to use a television in your house or flat, you *must* obtain a television licence.

You can buy a TV licence from any post office. It costs £22 if your television is black and white, and £66 if you have a colour television. It is illegal to use a television without a licence, and you might have to pay a fine if you are caught.

'Excuse me, could you help me with this plug?'

BRITAIN AND ITS PEOPLE

Britain, along with Northern Ireland, makes up what is called the **United Kingdom.** Britain itself consists of three different countries. **England, Scotland** and **Wales.**

Although the four countries of the United Kingdom make up one political and economic unit, each country tries to keep its own character and identity. Wales, in fact, has its own language and many Welsh people speak both Welsh and English.

Although it is part of what is referred to as **The British Isles,** Southern Ireland (Eire) is a separate country with its own government. If you go to Southern Ireland, you are leaving the United Kingdom and therefore need your passport and all the other documents you need to leave and re-enter the United Kingdom.

The geography of Britain

Britain may be small but it has a very varied landscape. There is flat countryside in the east of England, mountains and forests in Wales and Scotland and lakes in the far north of England (called the **Lake District).** From any point in Britain you are never more than 75 miles (120 km) from the sea and a beautiful coastline. There are also still parts of Britain where you can find yourself in complete solitude. In fact, Britain has a surprising amount of countryside and open spaces, never very far away from any large town or city.

Politics

Britain is a **monarchy,** and its present monarch is **Queen Elizabeth II.** Although the monarch is the head of the government, she has very little real political power. Laws are made and changed in **Parliament.** Parliament consists of two sections, the **House of Commons** (members are elected) and the **House of Lords** (members are not elected; membership is mostly hereditary). The House of Commons is where most of the laws are originally made. The function of the House of Lords is largely to revise and amend laws.

The House of Commons consists of 650 Members of Parliament (MPs), who have been elected by the people of Britain. Each Member of Parliament usually belongs to a political party. The four main political parties in Britain are **Conservative, Labour, Liberal Democratic** and **Social Democratic,** although there are quite a few others. The political party which has the most representatives in the House of Commons forms the **government,** and the leader of that political party becomes the **Prime Minister.** Elections for parliament take place every five years, unless the Prime Minister wants an earlier election.

The administration of local matters — for example traffic, roads, police, schools and health — is dealt with by **local government** or **local authorities.** Local governments are also run by elected members.

Many British people feel that their political opinions are private and do not discuss them, even amongst friends. Others have very strong opinions which can turn a discussion into a violent argument. Don't talk about politics with someone until you know them very well.

Towns and cities

Many of the large cities in Britain are commercial or industrial and often consist of a mixture of old and new buildings. Some cities, like **Bath** for example, are extremely old and have many examples of remains of Roman buildings. Other cities, like **Milton Keynes**, have been built in recent years and only have modern buildings.

Many of the towns and cities in Britain are still very beauitful. Most have rivers running through their centre, a cathedral and a selection of churches and buildings of historical or architectural interest. Some still have remains of ancient castles.

Buildings are usually made from whatever material is found locally. This may be brick, stone, granite, flint, wood, sandstone or even a combination of materials. This means that as you travel through Britain, you will find that each area has its own distinctive appearance.

Climate

The climate in Britain is never really hot, rarely above 30°C. Summer is supposed to be between June and September, although this cannot be guaranteed! The average July temperature in the south of England is 17°C. In Winter (late November to March), the temperature can reach below 0°C. For most of the year, the temperature is mild but the climate tends to be damp. The only sure thing anyone can say about the British weather is that it is very changeable!

The weather and temperature also depend on where in Britain you are living. The north is usually colder and damper than the south, and the south west gets more rain than the south east.

Clothes

You will need to bring quite a lot of warm and waterproof clothing.

If you come from a country where warm clothes are far more

expensive to buy than in Britain, buy as much of your warm clothing
as possible in Britain. You will have less luggage to carry. You will
also have the opportunity to see what sort of things everyone else is
wearing.

If you are flying from a hot country, carry one item of warm
clothing, such as a jumper or a jacket, in your hand luggage. You
will need to put this on when you get off the plane. Carry a small
umbrella as well.

Most British students wear very casual clothes for attending college.
However, bring at least *one* set of smart clothes for any formal
occasions which you want to attend.

Public holidays and festivals
There are eight public holidays, usually referred to as **bank holidays,**
in Britain. As well as these, there are a few more which just apply
to people living in Scotland and Northern Ireland. On bank holidays
most offices, including banks, shops and schools, are closed.

Bank holidays
— **New Year's Day**	1st January
— **New Year's Bank Holiday**	2nd January (Scotland only)
— **St. Patrick's Day**	17th March (Ireland only)
— **Good Friday**	The Friday before Easter Sunday (the date changes each year)
— **Easter Monday**	The Monday after Easter Sunday (the date changes), (not Scotland)
— **May Day Holiday**	The first Monday in May
— **Spring Bank Holiday**	The last Monday in May
— **Battle of the Boyne**	12th July (Ireland only)
— **Summer Bank Holiday**	The last Monday in August
— **Christmas Day**	25th December
— **Boxing Day**	26th December

Lent
Lent is a period of 40 days leading up to Easter. During Lent people
take part in a variety of religious and non-religious activities and
events. **Shrove Tuesday** (sometimes known as pancake day) is the
day you traditionally eat pancakes. The fourth Sunday of Lent is
Mother's Day, when children give their mothers flowers, gifts and
greeting cards. **Maundy Thursday,** the Thursday before Easter, is
when the Queen gives special coins to a selection of elderly people.

Good Friday, Easter Sunday and Easter Monday are the three main
days of Easter. As Easter is a religious festival, many British people

go to church (on Easter Sunday), but, like Christmas, the main emphasis is on the family. Families go out together, some towns have Easter parades, and people give children chocolate eggs.

Halloween — 31st October
On this day children dress up as witches, ghosts and so on. People sometimes have Halloween parties, where traditional Halloween games are played.

Guy Fawkes night — 5th November
Guy Fawkes night celebrates the discovery of a plot to blow up the Houses of Parliament in 1605. On Guy Fawkes night, people light **bonfires** and let off **fireworks** in their gardens or go to parks where there are public firework displays.

Several weeks before Guy Fawkes night you may see children in the street, or even coming to your house, carrying a replica of Guy Fawkes and asking for "a penny for the guy." They are asking for money to buy fireworks.

Christmas
The **Christmas** season begins very early in Britain. By the end of October you may see Christmas decorations in the streets and Christmas cards and gifts in the shops.

Traditionally, people start to decorate their houses a week or two before 25th December, which is Christmas Day. To decorate for Christmas people hang up holly, tinsel, balloons and bring a Christmas tree into the house. This is usually a small pine tree, decorated with coloured ornaments and lights. At around the same time, people send each other special Christmas greeting cards.

On 24th December, which is called **Christmas Eve,** children hang up 'stockings' (usually pillow cases) which they hope will be filled with presents by **Father Christmas** or **Santa Claus** during the night. Many people go to church just before midnight, to join in a **Midnight Mass.**

Christmas Day itself is celebrated in different ways in different households. It is usually a time when families get together. Some go to church on Christmas morning, and gifts are exchanged. Special Christmas meals are eaten, and friends are visted.

New Year's Eve — 31st December
On the night of 31st December, most people stay up until at least just after midnight in order to "see in" the New Year. This is a very

popular night to have a party, and it is also the night of the year when most pubs, bars and restaurants forget about their usual closing times and stay open until after midnight.

In London, thousands of people go to **Trafalgar Square** to hear **Big Ben** (the clock next to the Houses of Parliament) chime midnight. This can be fun but it can also be unpleasant if you dislike large crowds of people. In Scotland, New Year's Eve is called **Hogmanay** and is a much more important occasion than in the rest of Britain.

Birthdays
In Britain, when it is your birthday, friends and relatives usually give you greeting cards and gifts and sometimes birthday cake. Some people have parties, others choose to celebrate their birthday by going on an outing or going to a special restaurant.

The people
British people have always had a reputation for being cold and reserved. It would be more accurate to say that British people are very private. Britain is very much an 'indoor society' and this is probably because of the climate. People living in warmer countries lead a much more outdoor life, and therefore less private life, than people from cooler climates.

British people also find it difficult to show emotion in public. It is very unusual to see British people arguing, embracing (especially men), crying, even being extremely happy in public places. Usually they are more inhibited and modest. However, it is misleading to generalise about a group of people who are so diverse.

You may find that British people take a long time to get to know, but once you do, you will find that most of them are as warm and friendly as anyone else.

Meals in a British home
Mealtimes for the British, perhaps with the exception of younger people, follow quite a fixed pattern.

Breakfast is usually eaten between **7.00** and **8.00am** and will probably consist of cereal with milk followed by toast. It is quite rare to find people eating a 'traditional English breakfast' of bacon, eggs and sausages, except perhaps at weekends.

Lunch (as it is called in some parts of Britain) and **dinner** (as it is called in other parts) is the mid-day meal and can be anything from a sandwich to a three course meal. The evening meal is either called **dinner** or **tea**. If you are invited for tea, don't just expect to be given a drink. Tea is often a light meal eaten in the late afternoon or early evening. Many people regard eating out in restaurants as a luxury.

People often socialise at home, but unless you know someone very well it is not usual to 'drop in' (visit) without being invited. If you *are* invited to someone's house for a meal, it is customary to take a small gift such as a bottle of wine, flowers or chocolates.

Family life
You may find family life in Britain very different from family life in your home country. Although family ties are usually quite strong, it is not usual to find whole families, including grandparents, aunts and cousins, living together in the same house, or even in the same town.

In general, if a young person leaves his or her home town to go away to college, they very rarely come back to the same town at the end of their course. Many get married and set up their own home or move to where they think they will be able to get a job.

Pets
Many British families have at least one **pet**, a tame animal, which lives in the house with them and which they treat as part of the family. **Dogs** and **cats** are favourite types of pets but you will also find birds, goldfish, rabbits, hamsters and even mice!

BRITAIN AS A MULTI-RACIAL SOCIETY

The population of Britain is made up of people from many different races and nationalities. In some towns and cities, you will find that people of the same race often group together, living in the same areas, forming small communities of their own, and maintaining the culture and traditions of their countries of origin. Within these communities you will find social clubs, religious centres, shops and restaurants selling traditional foods and items.

As a visitor from overseas, you will not feel at all out of place, especially if you are living in a large town or city. As well as the many people from overseas who have settled in Britain, you will also find many other students from overseas, tourists and business people visiting Britain. In some smaller towns and villages you may find people who are still not quite so used to meeting people from overseas, and who might regard you as something of a novelty.

Prejudice
Few people can truthfully say that they have *never* been prejudiced

against something or someone. Prejudice comes from ignorance, and from not understanding differences between cultures or groups of people. It becomes worse when you start to judge the differences, and confuse what is different with what is better or worse.

Many people in Britain already have opinions about people from other countries. These opinions might be based on previous encounters with foreigners, or on something read in newspapers, from watching television or listening to what other people have told them. The opinions people have, however, are often based on misunderstandings, exaggerations or lies.

Unfortunately, there are *a few* people in Britain who:

- believe that their ways are better than everyone else's;
- think that people from overseas should adopt British ways of doing things while they are in Britain, and give up their 'foreign' ways;
- believe that they are doing you a favour by providing you with the opportunity of studying in Britain;
- might treat you as if you are inferior to them because you speak English with a different accent from them.

In many communities, people from different racial groups or different religions manage to live happily and peacefully together. Unfortunately, however, there is a small amount of **racism** in Britain, which is antagonism or even violence towards people of a different race.

Racism

Racism can appear in many ways. You may experience any of the following:

- People behaving badly towards you;
- People deliberately putting obstacles in your way — for example, not giving you a room in a house, or a job;
- Physical violence.

In Britain, *all* types of discrimination against people on the grounds of their race are unlawful.

If you experience such discrimination, report it either to your local **Community Relations Council** or to the local branch of the **Commission for Racial Equality** (you will find their addresses in your local *Yellow Pages* telephone directory). You may not feel that reporting an incident will help you in any way, but it may help others.

WOMEN IN BRITISH SOCIETY

By law, women in Britain have the same rights as men. This includes equal opportunities for jobs and equal pay for equal work. *It is against the law to discriminate against someone because she is a woman.*

In large towns and cities, where there are usually more single people, it is quite usual for women to go out to bars, restaurants, cinemas and so on, in pairs, in groups and sometimes alone. Unfortunately, there are still some people who think that women out alone want male company. In fact, the majority of women who go out together are quite happy in each other's company, and will resent being disturbed by groups of men looking for female company.

IN TROUBLE WITH THE LAW

If you are ever arrested by the police, or sent for trial at a court of law, it is very important that you get **professional advice** from one of the following:

● the welfare officer at your college
● your college student union
● the National Union of Students
● a Citizens Advice Bureau
● a Law Centre

Being **convicted**, found guilty, of a crime can have serious implications for a visitor from overseas. It means that:

● A record of what has happened is kept in your Home Office file.
● In the future, it will be more difficult to apply for an extension of your leave to remain, or for a visa.
● If you have committed a very serious offence, you could be deported.

Arrests

The police have the power to stop, search and arrest anyone who appears to be acting suspiciously or who is seen committing an offence.

If you are arrested:

● *Don't* be aggressive, but try to be as **polite** as possible, even if you don't feel like being polite.
● *Don't* try to bribe the police or make any deals with them.
● *Don't* refuse to give your name and address. You are obliged, by

law, to provide this information if asked and refusing could make matters worse.

● *Don't* sign a statement until you have received advice from a **solicitor**.
● If you are arrested by **plain clothes police**, who don't wear a police uniform, ask to see some form of identification.

Help

If you are arrested, you are entitled to make one phonecall. If you make this call to a friend, tell your friend to contact someone from your college, from the student union or from a Citizens Advice Bureau, to tell them what has happened and to get advice about what to do.

Solicitors

If you are going to appear in court, you *must* be represented by a solicitor (or a barrister if your case is going to a high court). The local Citizens Advice Bureau or Law Centre can put you in touch with a solicitor.

Legal aid

The Citizens Advice Bureau will also tell you if you are entitled to **legal aid**, which can help to pay for the solicitor's fees. Legal aid is **means tested**, which means you can get legal aid if your income is not very large. It is better to contact a Citizens Advice Bureau *before* going directly to a solicitor because some Bureaux have their own solicitors who will give their services free of charge.

Interpreters

If you have to go to court, and you are worried about whether your English is good enough to understand everything that is going on, you can ask for an **interpreter**. The court will provide one for you if you require, or you can find one of your own. It is better to get someone you know if possible.

Offences

Criminal offences are similar throughout the world, only the forms of punishment may be different. The most common form of punishment in Britain is a **fine**. This is when the court orders you to pay a sum of money. For serious offences, the penalty will be **imprisonment**.

If you are caught committing a criminal offence, don't plead ignorance of the law. This is not accepted as an excuse.

Shoplifting

The penalty for **shoplifting** (stealing goods from shops) can be a very large fine. Sometimes shoplifters are sent to prison.

When you are in shops, don't put anything you have not yet paid for into your pocket or your bag. Even if you only intend to leave it there for a few minutes, you may forget about it and walk out of the shop without paying for it. If anyone has seen you do this they won't believe you when you say you did not *intend* to steal it.

In large stores and supermarkets you are provided with a wire basket. Always take this basket around the store and use it to carry everything you want to buy.

Possession of an offensive weapon

Offensive weapons include flick-knives, other knives, guns and studded belts. In Britain, it is illegal to carry an offensive weapon and if you are caught doing so you will probably have to pay a fine.

Drugs

The authorities regard the possession of *small* quantities of cannabis, if you are not selling it, as a fairly minor offence and the penalty will normally be a small fine.

If you are carrying or using **hard drugs** (for example, cocaine, heroin) or *supplying any* drugs, including cannabis, you will probably have to go to prison. This is regarded as a very serious offence in Britain.

Criminal damage

Any form of **vandalism**, damage to public or private property, is an offence. The penalty for this is usually a fine. You will probably also have to pay for any repairs which have to be made. Vandalism includes damaging telephone boxes, breaking windows, damaging parked cars, and writing graffiti on walls.

Disorderly conduct

You can be arrested for any form of rowdy or excessively noisy behaviour. This is called **disorderly conduct**.

Driving when under the influence of alchohol

This is a very serious offence and offenders have to pay **very heavy fines** (up to £1000). If you are convicted of this offence you will also be banned from driving for one year or more.

Other motoring offences

Examples of these are: **reckless driving, driving without insurance, driving under age,** and **breaking the traffic laws.** All motoring offences result in a fine and the possibility of being banned from driving.

If you are in trouble for committing a motoring offence, don't try to say that you are from overseas and are unfamiliar with the British regulations. The authorities expect you to know regulations *before* you drive on British roads.

THE POLICE

The police in Britain are not connected in any way to the army. They are there to make sure that British laws are kept, and also to help and protect the general public. If you find yourself in any trouble, don't be afraid call the police for help.

In Britain, one police force deals with all areas of the law, including traffic law. The police are usually unarmed. They carry **truncheons,** small wooden or leather batons, but only carry guns in special circumstances. Policemen are often called **the cops** or **bobbys.**

OFFENCES AGAINST YOU

If someone has committed an offence against you, you might still have to go to court to give evidence against them. Go to a local Citizens Advice Bureau for advice first.

Theft

- When you are out, *always* carry your money in an **inaccessible place** (not your back pocket).
- If you carry a bag, keep it **closed.**
- *Never* leave bags or coats **unattended**.
- *Don't* put your purse or wallet down on a shop counter or on a table in a restaurant. Always keep it in your hand.
- *Never* keep your keys in the same place as something with your address written on it.
- It is probably a good idea to keep your passport at home. In Britain, you don't have to carry identification with you at all times, although you need it for some things, such as cashing travellers cheques.

Always report theft to the police, even if it is only a small incident.

Assault

- Don't take short cuts through dark, secluded places.
- Walk confidently.
- Walk in the middle of the pavement.
- Walk towards on-coming traffic.
- Don't get into empty train compartments on your own.
- If you think you are being followed, walk up to the nearest lighted house and ask someone to let you in.
- If someone attacks you, scream, shout, kick and make as much noise as you can.
- If someone is attacking you, you can *legally* use reasonable force against them in self defence.

Rape

If you are raped or sexually assaulted, *it is your decision* whether or not to go to the police. If you decide to go to the police, go as soon as possible after the event. You will have to have an internal examination and answer detailed questions about your private life as well as the assault itself. Don't be surprised if you feel like the person accused of the crime. It is your *right* to ask to be examined by a female doctor.

Many large towns and cities have a **Rape Crisis Centre,** where you can go for help and advice. If you want someone to go to the police with you, they will provide this service. The 24 hour telephone number of the London Rape Crisis Centre is (01) 837 1600.

Compensation

If someone has assaulted you, violently attacked and injured you, you may be able to get financial compensation, *even if the person has not been caught by the police.*

If this has happened to you, contact **The Criminal Injuries Compensation Board,** 19 Alfred Place, London WC1. Tel: (01) 636 9501.

Emergencies

To call the police in an emergency, go to any phone and dial 999. The operator will ask, 'Which service do you require?' You then have the choice of the police, ambulance or fire services. This call is free.

7
Travel in Britain

Your first experience of travel in Britain will be from the airport or seaport where you landed. For many, the first journey is from Heathrow or Gatwick airport to central London to catch a train or bus to another part of Britain. If you have arrived at one of Britain's other airports, or a seaport, you may be able to avoid central London and travel directly to your destination.

Your school or college should have sent you directions for the best way of travelling there from your port of entry. If they don't, write and ask them for directions, or write to the British Tourist Authority (see Appendix 6). It will be much easier if you have planned your route before you arrive in Britain.

If, at any point on your journey, you are not sure where to go, or how to get there, look for the information centre which you will find at all airports, seaports and major stations by following these signs:

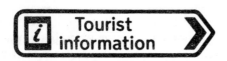 

TRAVEL FROM HEATHROW AIRPORT TO CENTRAL LONDON

Heathrow airport is about 17 miles (27 kilometres) from central London. It is situated to the south-west of the city.

The underground
The quickest way of getting from Heathrow to central London is by

underground (the **tube**). The journey takes about 50 minutes and currently costs £1.90. Trains run about every 5 minutes from 5.00am to 11.45pm, Monday to Saturday, and from 6.45am to 11.00pm on Sundays. To find the underground, look for signs like this:

Before you can buy a ticket, you must decide where you are going. Use one of the large underground maps which look like the one on page 140.

The underground has nine different **lines**. Each line has a name, and is shown in a different colour on the map.

Heathrow is on the **Piccadilly Line,** which is dark blue. If your destination is *not* on the Piccadilly line, you will have to change lines during your journey. You do this by getting off the train at a station where the Piccadilly line crosses the line you want.

If you need to travel to one of London's main railway stations to continue your journey by train, the chart on page 145 will show you which railway station you might need.

Tickets

If you have some coins, you can buy your ticket from a **ticket machine.** *Some* machines will give you change if you don't have the right coins, but some do not give change, so check before putting money into the machine. If you don't have any coins, go to the **ticket office.**

Once you have bought your ticket you can enter the underground, either by going through an **automatic gate** or by walking past the **ticket inspector.** If you have a lot of luggage don't try to go through the automatic gate.

To open the gate, put the ticket into the slot then, when the gate opens, walk through. *Don't forget to pick up your ticket at the other side of the gate*, as you will need to show it when you leave the underground.

Entering the underground

Unfortunately, this is where you have to leave your luggage trolley and start carrying your luggage. Most underground stations have

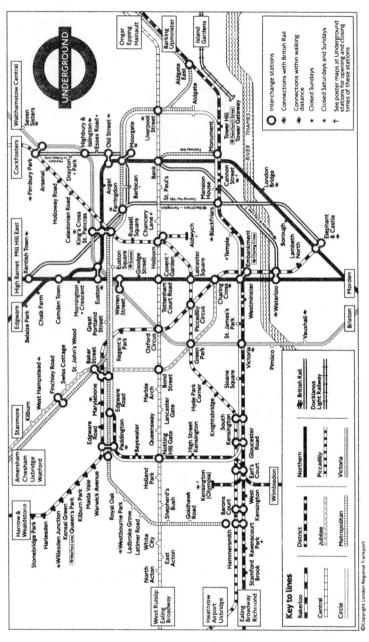

A map showing details of London's Underground System.
(LRT Registered User No. 89/1055)

escalators (moving stairways) which take you down to the trains. These are not very easy if you have a lot of luggage. If you can, try to stand, and keep all your luggage, *on the left hand side* of the escalator, leaving a space for people in a hurry to walk past. If you are blocking the way you will probably find people pushing past you, grumbling or even shouting at you.

Travelling on the underground during **rush hour** (8.00 — 10.00am and 4.30 — 6.30pm), which is when most people travel to and from work, is not a very pleasant experience. The trains are packed with people and it is almost impossible to get a seat, so you have to stand up and be squashed against the person standing next to you. Everyone is in a hurry and most people are in a bad mood.

The bus

If you prefer, you can take a **bus** from Heathrow airport to central London. Although the bus will take longer than the underground (between one hour, and one hour 30 minutes), it is easier if you are carrying a lot of luggage.

The bus is a red **double-decker** (a bus with an upstairs and downstairs) and is called **Airbus**. A1 Airbus goes to Victoria railway station and A2 Airbus goes to Euston railway station. To catch the bus, wait at the Airbus bus stop which you will find outside each passenger terminal. You can buy your ticket on the bus. It costs £4.

The Airbus runs (every 20-30 minutes) between 6.30am and 9.30pm. At any other time you should catch **Nightbus N97** which leaves from the **Central Bus Station** (this is situated between Terminals one and two, in front of the Queen's building). From the Central Bus Station, you can also get a bus or coach to many other towns and cities in the south of England. There is also a bus which will take you to Gatwick or Luton airport, if you have a connecting flight.

If you prefer travelling by train, you can avoid central London by taking a **Greenline** bus from Heathrow to **Reading** railway station (less than an hour) and then taking a train. Trains from Reading will take you to destinations in the south of England, including: Bath, Birmingham, Bournemouth, Bristol, Coventry, Dover, Exeter, Gloucester, Guildford, Oxford, Penzance, Plymouth, Portsmouth, Southampton, South Wales, Torquay, Winchester.

TRAVEL FROM GATWICK AIRPORT

Gatwick airport is about 30 miles (50 kilometres) south of London. A train called the **Gatwick Express** will take you from the airport to Victoria railway station in central London. These trains run every fifteen minutes during the day, every half hour between 10.30pm and 01.00am and every hour throughout the night. The journey takes about thirty minutes, and costs £5.

To find the train at the airport, look for signs like this:

This is the symbol for British Rail, Britain's only national rail network.

If your final destination is towards the *south-east* of England, (for example, Brighton, Chichester, Eastbourne, Maidstone, Reading, Worthing), the north-west of England or the midlands (for example, Birmingham, Coventry, Crewe, Liverpool, Manchester), you can avoid travelling to central London and take a train or coach directly from Gatwick.

TRAVEL FROM LUTON AIRPORT

Luton airport is about 33 miles (52 kilometres) north of central London.

A train and coach service called the **Luton Flyer** will take you from Luton airport, via Luton railway station, to **St. Pancras** railway station in central London.

The coach leaves the airport, outside the departures terminal, every hour throughout the night and every half-hour between 9.07am and 10.37pm. Buy your ticket from the arrivals lounge in the airport terminal. It costs £6.

You can also travel from Luton railway station to destinations in the north and north-east of Britain, or take a **National Express Coach,** from Luton bus station, to many large towns and cities in Britain.

TRAVEL FROM SEA PORTS

All major sea ports have trains running to central London. You may also be able to avoid London, and travel directly from the port to your final destination. At the port look out for the British Rail sign which shows you where to catch the train.

Taxis

If you are travelling from one of London's international airports to central London, don't take a taxi unless you are extremely rich! The *minimum* fare from Heathrow, the airport nearest to central London, is about £25. If you are travelling in a group of four people, and each of you has a lot of luggage, you may feel that it would be worth paying for a taxi.

Taxi in central London

If you simply want to cross London from one railway station to another, or from a station to your hotel, then a taxi might be a good idea. Although taxis may seem quite expensive, they make life a lot easier if you have a lot of luggage, or if you are not confident about finding your way around the underground system. Here are some useful facts about using taxis:

● Licensed taxis are large, and usually black, vehicles with a small white plate on the back showing a licence number and the words **Hackney Carriages.**

● The best place to find a taxi is at a railway station. Follow the signs for taxi and you will find what is called a **taxi rank** (a place in the road where taxis can stop), and probably a queue of people waiting for taxis.

● Another good place to find a taxi is near a large hotel.

● If you are not at a station, you will have to stand in the street and wait for one to go past. Look for a taxi which has an orange light lit up over the driver's window — this means that it is not being used by anyone else.

● When the taxi is quite close, raise your arm and wave to the driver. The taxi should then stop for you.

● When you pay, it is usual to give the driver a tip of about 10%.

Taxis at your destination

When you arrive at your final destination, take a local taxi from the station to the college. You will usually find taxis waiting outside the station entrance.

TRAVEL FROM LONDON TO OTHER PARTS OF BRITAIN

If your final destination is *not* London, you'll probably have to travel there from one of London's railway or coach stations. Travel by train is quicker than coach travel, but it is more expensive.

Travel by train

The map on page 147 shows the train network throughout Britain. All trains are run by one company, **British Rail**.

The chart below will give you some idea of which railway station in London you should use to get to your final destination. Before you travel, you should telephone the station to get information about the times of the trains.

Before you get on a train, buy a ticket from the ticket office in the station. When you buy your ticket you will have the choice of either **first class** or **second class**. A first class ticket is about 50% more expensive than a second class ticket. Most people in Britain travel by second class, and you will find a second class seat quite comfortable. For more information about tickets and prices, see page 50.

A ticket for a journey on a train does *not*, however, guarantee a seat. On very crowded trains, some people may have to stand for the whole journey. If you want to be sure of a seat, you can make a **seat reservation** when you buy your ticket. The seat reservation costs £1. You will be given a separate ticket which tells you where you will find

Which train station do I need?

Destinations	Station
Birmingham, Chester, Coventry, Crewe, Glasgow, Lancaster, Liverpool, Manchester, Northampton, Preston, Stoke-on-Trent, Wolverhampton.	Euston (01) 387 7070
Bedford, Derby, Leicester, Luton, Nottingham, Sheffield.	St. Pancras (01) 387 7070
Aberdeen, Bradford, Darlington, Doncaster, Dundee, Hull, Edinburgh, Leeds, Newcastle, Peterborough, York.	Kings Cross (01) 278 2477
Cambridge, Colchester, Ipswich, Kings Lynn, Norwich.	Liverpool Street (01) 283 7171
Bath, Bristol, Cardiff, Exeter, Oxford, Penzance, Plymouth, Reading, South Wales.	Paddington (01) 262 6767
Basingstoke, Bournemouth, Guildford, Isle of Wight, Portsmouth, Salisbury, Southampton, Weymouth, Winchester.	Waterloo (01) 928 5100
Canterbury, Dover, Margate, Ramsgate.	Charing Cross (01) 928 5100
Bognor, Brighton, Chichester, Eastbourne, Gatwick, Maidstone, Worthing.	Victoria (01) 928 5100

your seat. For example, *Carriage H Seat 24B,* or *Carriage G Seat 24F.*
F means that your seat is facing the engine, *B* means that you will be
travelling with your back to the engine.

When you find your seat, you will see that it has on it a card
marked **reserved.** If you have not reserved a seat, don't sit in any
seat which has a reserved card attached to it.

Most trains, except on short distances, have a **Buffet Car,** which is
where you can go to buy drinks and food. On some trains, someone
will come round with a trolley, selling drinks and food so you do not
have to leave your seat.

Finally, when you wish to get off the train, don't worry if you can't find a handle on the door! On many trains, the door handle is on the outside, so you have to open the window, reach out and open the door from the outside.

Young Persons Railcard
You can buy a **Young Persons Railcard** if:

● if you are *over* the age of 24; *or*
● if you do not have an International Student Identity card.

A Young Persons Railcard costs £15 and lasts for one year. With the card, you can get a **33%—50%** reduction off any train ticket you buy. If you intend to travel around Britain a lot, it's a good idea to buy one of these cards. If you are a student, you can also buy the card:

● if you are *over* the age of 24; *or*
● if you do not have an International Student Identity card.

However, you will have to wait until you have enrolled at your college, as British Rail will ask you to complete a form and provide a photograph of yourself, both signed by someone at your college.

Travel by coach
Long distance buses are called **coaches.** Some of the more modern ones are quite luxurious. Many provide drinks and snacks, show videos and have toilets on board.

The main coach station in London is called **Victoria coach station,** and is near Victoria railway station. From there, you can get a coach to most large towns in Britain, and also information about coaches from London. Tel: (01) 730 0202, or contact **National Express,** 13 Regent Street, London SW1 9TP Tel: (01) 824 8461. Of course, you don't have to be in London to get a coach. Most major towns and cities have coach stations from where you can travel around Britain.

Before you travel, buy a ticket from the ticket office at the coach station. If you have an International Student Identity Card, you can buy a **Student Coach Card** which will give you up to a 33% reduction off all fares. The card costs £4 and lasts for one year.

If you don't have the International Student Identity Card, you have to prove that you are a student by asking someone at your college to sign the application form.

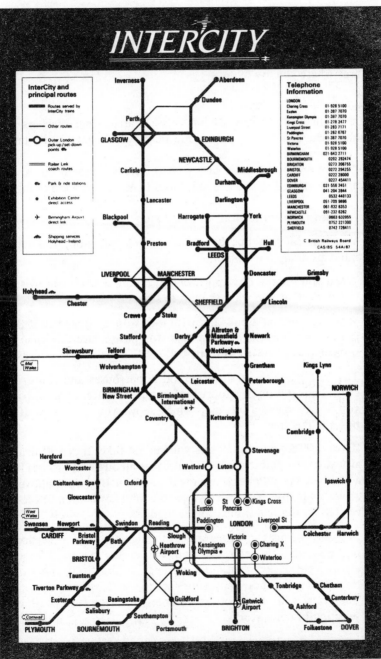

A map showing the main train lines of Britain.
(Licence No. TLB/89/2104)

Local public transport

You'll probably need to use some form of local transport, either to get to and from college every day, to visit friends or to see more of the area where you are living.

Buses

There might be two types of bus in your area; **single deckers** and **double deckers.** Double deckers are buses which have stairs inside and seats upstairs.

Different areas of Britain also have different coloured buses. For example, buses in London are red, buses in Manchester are orange.

Useful things to remember about buses

- You can catch a bus by standing at a bus stop, situated at intervals along the bus route.

- When you see the bus approaching, hold out your arm to show the driver that you want the bus to stop.

- When you are on a bus, and wish it to stop, ring the bell if there is one, or call to the driver, 'Next stop please.' Do this plenty of time before the next bus stop.

- The best place to get information about buses and routes is a central bus station or a tourist information centre. In many towns you will be given a bus map which shows you the routes of the buses in the area.

- If you ask anyone which bus you should take, they will usually give you the number of the bus, because all buses and routes have a number. The number is usually on the front of the bus above the driver's window. You will also see the final destination of the bus written on the front, next to the number.

- In many towns the buses are changing from old style double deckers, with the entrance and exit at the back, to modern style single deckers with the entrance at the front and exit in the middle. On these, pay your fare to the driver as you get on. The driver will often not accept notes, so make sure you have a selection of coins ready.

- In most large towns and cities, you can buy a bus pass or season ticket. In some you will be able to buy a daily bus pass, in others a weekly or monthly one. These are often worth buying because:

— you can get on and off as many buses as you want;
— if you use the buses a lot, they are cheaper than paying for each separate journey;
— you don't have to keep looking for coins to pay your fare.

For information about bus passes or season tickets, go to the central bus station or to a tourist information centre.

● In London, you can buy something called a Travel Card, which you can use on the buses and on the Underground. You can buy a daily weekly, monthly or annual travel card, from any underground station.

Local trains

As well as the **Intercity** networks of trains (see page 147), Britain also has a good local train network. The local trains, like the intercity trains, are run by British Rail.

For information about local trains, go to the railway station nearest to where you live and ask for a timetable of trains and a map showing the routes of the local trains. If you are going to use a particular route regularly, you should buy a **season ticket.** If you have a Young Persons Railcard (see page 146), you can buy your season ticket at a reduced price.

Unlike Intercity trains, not all local trains have toilets on board, and very few sell food and drinks on the train.

Driving

To drive a car or a motorcycle in Britain you must have a valid licence and you must be at least 17 years old (16 for mopeds).

For the first year you are in Britain, you can use your overseas driving licence. If you are going to stay in Britain for longer than one year, you *might* have to go back to being a **learner driver** and take a driving test in Britain, depending on where you come from. This means you must:

● apply for a provisional licence (obtain the form at any post office, the licence costs £17);
● display 'L' plates (a 'learner' sign) on your car or motorcycle;
● not drive the car without being accompanied by someone who has a full driving licence;
● not ride a motorcycle which is more powerful than 125cc, or carry a passenger on a motorcycle;
● have some driving lessons, which currently cost about £12 an hour;

- learn *The Highway Code* (the driver's rulebook);
- take a driving test which currently costs £43 (enrol as soon as possible as there is always a long waiting list).

If you are from the EC, or from a country which has a special agreement with Britain, you may not have to take a test. You can simply exchange your own licence for a British one. Check with the AA or RAC (see page 152) to see of this applies to you.

If you are going to drive in Britain, you *must* obtain a copy of The *Highway Code*. This is the book which contains all the rules and regulations concerning driving and vehicles. The police in Britain are quite strict about motoring offences and ignorance of the law is *not* accepted as an excuse for committing an offence. You will also be tested on the highway code during your driving test. You can obtain a copy of The Highway Code from most bookshops.

'No, no! The LEFT hand side of the road!'

Useful points about driving in Britain
- You must drive on the **left-hand side** of the road.
- You must overtake on the **right**.
- The driver of a car, and the passenger sitting in the front seat, must wear **seat belts**. Children riding in the back must also wear seat belts if they are available.

- If you ride a motorcycle or moped, you must wear a **crash helmet.**
- If you have been drinking **alcohol,** do not drive. If you are caught driving under the influence of alcohol, you will lose your licence.
- You are not allowed to park your car where there is a **double yellow line** drawn along the side of the road.
- Where there is a **single yellow line,** it means that you can park there only at certain times. These times are shown on a nearby sign.
- The **speed limit** in Britain is 30 miles per hour (48 km/h) in towns, 60 miles per hour (96 km/h) on open roads and 70 miles per hour (112 km/h) on motorways. Speed limits are shown by black numbers in a red circle.

Signs indicating the speed limits on English roads – remember, the
numbers indicate miles per hour, *not* kilometres.
(Crown copyright. Reproduced with the permission of
the Controller of Her Majesty's Stationery Office.)

If you buy a car

Running a car in Britain is quite expensive. Any car which you buy must have **tax, insurance** and, if it is a second-hand car over three years old, **MOT.**

Tax

In Britain, everyone who owns a car must pay a **road tax.** This tax costs £100 per year. To tax your car, you must complete a form, which is available at any post office, and send it to the tax office along with the correct payment. You can either pay tax for a whole year or for six months at a time. It takes several weeks to receive a reply.

You will then be sent a circular paper disc which must be displayed in the front window of your car. It is an offence to drive a car which does not display the tax disc.

Insurance

The cost of insuring a car depends on:

- how old you are;
- how long you have been driving;
- the type of car you have;
- the amount of insurance cover you require.

Insurance can cost at least £100 per year, probably much more. Endsleigh Insurance Services offers a car insurance scheme for students. Their address is Cranfield House, 97–107 Southampton Row, London WC1B 4AG. Tel: (01) 436 4451.

MOT

The MOT is the **Ministry of Transport roadworthiness test**. All cars over three years old must pass this test. The basic test costs about £13 at most garages, but if the car needs any work doing to it before it will pass the test, you will have to pay much more.

Motoring clubs

There are two motoring clubs in Britain, both of which provide invaluable information on driving, buying and looking after a car;

The Automobile Association (AA)
Fanum House
Basing View
Basingstoke
Hampshire RG21 2EA
Tel: (0256) 20123

The Royal Automobile Club (RAC)
83–85 Pall Mall
London SW1Y 5HW
Tel: (01) 839 7050

Some overseas motoring clubs have reciprocal arrangements with these two British clubs. If you are a member of a motoring club in your home country, check before you leave whether you are entitled to any benefits while you are in Britain.

Hiring a car

In order to hire a car you must:
- be over 21 years old (some companies require you to be over 23):
- have held a full driving licence for at least one year. (International

driving licences and *some* overseas licences are accepted.)

There are a lot of car-hire companies in Britain. To find one, the best place to look is in the *Yellow Pages* telephone directory.

Each car-hire firm will have slightly different terms and conditions, so investigate several to find the one which suits you own needs. Points to watch out for when hiring a car:

● Does the price depend on how far you are going to drive, or is it a fixed price with unlimited mileage? If you are hiring a car for a day, the price you are charged usually depends on how many miles you drive. Prices are usually between £18–£40 per day plus 10p–40p per mile. If you hire a car for a longer period you are usually given unlimited mileage. This means that you can travel as many miles as you like for a fixed price. Prices are usually between £90–£350 per week.

● Does the price include insurance? Is the insurance cover adequate for you?

BEING A TOURIST

While you are in Britain, you will probably want to see as much of the country as possible. Britain is not very large and it is not difficult to travel around. You can cover the 393 miles (632 km) from London to Edinburgh in Scotland, for example, in four and a half hours by train, one hour by plane or nine hours by coach.

The best source of information on where to go, what to see, where to stay and how to get there is **The British Tourist Authority.** Write to them for information or visit their centre in London (see Appendix 6). Each major town will also have its own tourist information centre. Look for the signs on page 138.

The British Tourist Authority can give you information about discount tourist travel tickets and cheap fares for students. If you have planned your travels before you leave your home country, you can buy a travel pass called a **Britrail Pass** which entitles you to unlimited rail travel for however many days you specify. The problem with this pass is that you cannot buy it in Britain, so you must get if from a travel agency in your home country.

As far as accommodation is concerned, Britain offers a wide range of inexpensive places to stay. Ask at the tourist information centres about **youth hostels, bed and breakfast (B&B),** and **guest houses.** Alternatively, write in advance to:

- The Youth Hostel Association (See Appendix 6):
- Bed and Breakfast (GB), PO Box 66, Henley on Thames, Oxfordshire RG9 1XS.

Travelling abroad
While you are a student, take advantage of the wide range of special **student discount schemes** and **student tickets** for travel abroad from Britain. If your college has a student union, they may also have a **student travel office.** If not, you can obtain information from the following organisations:

- **Transalpino,** 71–75 Buckingham Palace Road, London SW1W OQU. Tel: (01) 834 9656.
- **STA Travel,** 86 Old Brompton Road, London SW5 OEE. Tel (01) 581 8233.
- **USIT,** 52 Grosvenor Gardens, London SW1 OAG. Tel (01) 383 5337.
- **Eurolines,** Victoria Coach Station, London SW1 9TP. Tel: (01) 730 0202.

8
Your Health

Medical certificates

Students enrolled on certain courses, and students from certain countries, may need to produce a **medical certificate** or evidence of vaccinations when entering Britain. To find out whether this applies to you, check with the British Embassy or High Commission before leaving your home country.

Do I have to pay for medical treatment?

Britain has a subsidised health service, the **National Health Service (NHS)**, which provides free health care and treatment for people who are resident in Britain. You may also be entitled to free medical treatment from the NHS if you are in one of the following categories.

● If you are from an EC country.

● If you are from a country which has a **reciprocal health agreement** with Britain. These are:

Austria	Gibraltar	Poland
British Virgin Islands	Hong Kong	Portugal
Bulgaria	Hungary	Romania
Channel Islands	Iceland	St Helena
Czechoslovakia	Isle of Man	Sweden
Falklands	Malta	Turks and Caicos Islands
Finland	Montserrat	USSR
German Democratic Republic	New Zealand Norway	Yugoslavia

● If you are a student, from any country, who is enrolled on a course which will last for more than six months.

● If you have come to Britain with a work permit.

- If you have **refugee status** or **Exceptional Leave to Remain** (see Chapter 4).

- If you are the wife or child of someone who is in one of the categories listed above.

- Even if you are not in one of the categories listed above you *will* receive free treatment if you are taken to an accident, casualty or emergency department of a hospital.

If none of these categories applies to you, you will not be able to receive free medical treatment and you will have to pay for each visit to a doctor or dentist and for the cost of any treatment you receive. This can become very expensive, so take out a **medical insurance policy.**

It is probably cheaper to get a medical insurance policy from your home country. If you are unable to do this you can get one in Britain from:

- The post office at Heathrow airport;
- **Medisure,** c/o Norman Frizzel Associates Ltd, Frizzel House, County Gates, Poole, Dorset BH13 6BH;
- **Stuart and Verity,** 22 Market Square, St. Neots, Huntingdon PE19 2AJ.

Pre-existing conditions
If you already have a medical condition for which you were receiving treatment *before* arriving in Britain, you will *not* be entitled to free treatment by the NHS, unless you are a student enrolled on a course lasting *six months* or more.

Registering with a doctor
As soon as you can, **register** with a doctor. Don't wait until you are ill. If your college has its own student health centre, register there. Otherwise you must find, and register with, the doctor nearest to where you are living.

You can find out where your nearest doctor is by going to:

- the post office;
- the Citizens Advice Bureau;
- your local Family Practitioner Committee (address from post office or in telephone directory).

If you have problems finding a doctor who will accept you, go to the Citizens Advice Bureau.

In order to register with a doctor, all you have to do is to go to the doctor's surgery, ask to register and you will be given a form to fill in.

A few weeks after you have registered with a doctor, you will be sent your **medical card**. On this card will be your NHS number, which you will need, so don't lose it.

Not all doctors have the same surgery hours. When you register, check when your doctor's surgery is open. Also check whether or not you need to make an **appointment** to see a doctor. Some doctors only see people by appointment, except in emergencies.

If you are *very* ill, and cannot leave your home, you can get a doctor to come out to see you. If you need to do this, try to phone the doctor *before 10.00am,* unless it is a real emergency.

Emergencies

In an emergency you can either:

- phone your doctor;
- phone for an ambulance (Tel:999);
- get someone to take you to a hospital *casualty* or *emergency* department.

Prescriptions

A **prescription** is something you are given if the doctor wants you to take any pills or medicine. Take the prescription to any chemists shop, and they will provide you with what you need.

For each item you are given, the current charge is £2.60.

Dentists

Dentists advise that people should have their teeth checked about every six months. Dental treatment is not free. Everyone has to pay something towards the cost of dental treatment but if you are entitled to NHS treatment, you can also receive dental treatment at *reduced* costs.

Current Dental Charges	NHS Patient	Private Patient
Check-up	£3.15	£10-£14 (£24-£36 for new patients)
Two small fillings	£6.80	£19-£27
Two medium sized fillings	£14	£28-£40
Clean and Polish	£5.25	£16.50-£25

You don't have to register with a dentist. Ask someone to recommend a good dentist, then phone to make an appointment. Make sure that the dentist you are going to see *does* deal with NHS patients. Be careful, because some dentists *only* see private patients, who pay the full cost of their treatment.

When you go to your dentist, take your medical card with you, otherwise you have no proof that you are entitled to NHS treatment. If you have made an appointment and find that you cannot attend, tell the dentist at least twenty-four hours in advance, otherwise he will charge you.

Opticians
In Britain *everyone* must now pay for eye-tests. As the prices for both frames and lenses are probably much more expensive in Britain than in your home country, it's a good idea to buy spectacles before you come to Britain. If possible, bring a spare pair in case you break or lose one pair.

Typical charges

Eye test	Spectacles	Contact lenses
£10	From £17.50	£60-£70
	(but can be much more)	

If you wear contact lenses, make sure that you have an insurance policy for your lenses, in case you lose them.

Family planning
Family planning is the term used in Britain to refer to contraception.

All *women* who are staying in Britain for over six months are entitled to free contraceptives. You can obtain contraceptives and advice on contraceptives from either your own doctor or a special **Family Planning Clinic.** Find out where your nearest clinic is from your doctor or from the telephone directory.

You can buy some types of contraceptive from chemist shops. For other types of contraceptive, for example the pill, you will need a prescription from a doctor.

Hospitals
Except for emergencies, you cannot usually go to a hospital for treatment unless a doctor recommends that you should go. If a doctor thinks you need specialist treatment, he will give you a letter to take to a local hospital, explaining what your problem is. It is up to you

to make an appointment for consultation with a specialist.

If you need treatment, or even a stay in hospital, you will probably have to wait for some time before you can be admitted. Unless it is an emergency, waiting lists for treatment in hospitals are quite long.

Sex and sexually transmitted diseases

You may find that, in Britain, attitudes towards sex are very different to those in your home country. The decision whether or not to have sex with someone should be your own decision. If you need to seek help or advice, whether it is about sex, contraception or related health matters, seek *professional* advice. A professional adviser will not judge you, and their help will be free and confidential.

If you do decide to have sex with someone, always make sure that you are using some form of contraception, preferably a condom;
● to avoid an unwanted pregnancy;
● to avoid catching or spreading a sexually transmitted disease, such as AIDS.

Condoms are sold at all chemists, some supermarkets, and women can obtain them free from Family Planning Clinics.

If you think that you might have a sexually transmitted disease, contact your own doctor immediately or, if you prefer to see someone you have never met before, go to a **special clinic**. These clinics are often located within a hospital. You may have to phone several hospitals before you can find one, but don't be embarrassed, the person on the other end of the phone doesn't know who you are. *All* treatment for sexually transmitted diseases is free.

If you are worried about AIDS, or think that you may have AIDS, you should contact an organisation called **The Terrence Higgins Trust.** Tel: (01) 242 1010 or (01) 831 0330, 9am to 10pm, Monday to Friday.

Pregnancy

If you are worried that you may be pregnant, you should have a **pregnancy test** straightaway. You can buy home pregnancy tests from any chemist, so you can test yourself, but its a good idea to have the test carried out by a doctor.

Discovering that you are pregnant may cause many anxieties, doubts and practical problems which you feel that you are unable to deal with on your own. It is very important that you seek professional advice either from your doctor, your student counsellor or from one of the many special organisations which are there to give this sort of help, such as:

— The Brook Advisory Centre, 153a East Street, London SE17 2SD. Tel: (01) 708 1234 (see *Yellow Pages* directory for local centres).
— British Pregnancy Advice Service, 58 Petty France, London SW1H 9EU. Tel: (01) 222 0985 (see the *Yellow Pages* directory for local centres).

Being gay

If you are gay — homosexual — you may feel that you are totally alone in the world, but there are, in fact, thousands of gay men and women living in Britain. Unfortunately, however, prejudice and even violence against gay people is not uncommon.

If you are studying at a large university or polytechnic, there may be a 'Gay Society' run by the student union, where you will be able to meet other gay people. Many cities also have organisations which publish special newspapers for gay people or run something called a 'Gay Switchboard' (a telephone line providing help and information for gay people). These provide a useful link between you and other gay people living in your area.

In London, there is a 24 hour gay switchboard providing counselling and information for gay men and women. Tel: (01) 837 7324.

GENERAL HEALTH

Keeping warm

People from warmer countries who are in Britain for the first time may find it difficult to cope with the cold, wet and damp weather. Many people catch colds or flu in winter and these illnesses are quickly passed around. If you do catch a cold, the best thing to do is to stay in bed for a few days, keep as warm as possible and drink lots of hot drinks and fruit juice.

Although you may find that heating bills are expensive, don't economise on heating. You can also keep yourself warm by wearing lots of thin layers of clothing, rather than just one or two thick, heavy items. For example, a T-shirt worn under a shirt, with a jumper on top, and a jacket on top of that, will keep you warmer than if you wear just a shirt and a heavy coat.

Always add extra clothing when you go outside, especially if you are going out into the cold after being in a very warm room.

Get some gloves, a hat and a scarf to add to your layers. If you get wet, always change into dry clothes as soon as possible.

Healthy eating

You may have to do your own cooking for the first time in your life. Although you may not think so, cooking a healthy meal is not particularly time-consuming or difficult. It is also cheaper than eating in restaurants all the time. Fast foods, take-away meals and quick snacks are always tempting, but try to vary your diet by eating plenty of fresh fruit and vegetables as well. There are three basic cookery books which you might find useful:

The Paupers Cookery Book, by J Innes;
Bedsitter Cooking, by M Patten;
The Penguin Cookery Book, by B Nilson.

Exercise

As a student, you will probably spend a lot of time sitting down at a desk and leaning over books. This can be bad for you if it is not mixed with some exercise. There will be plenty of opportunities for you to participate in sports activities at your college, so make the most of them. If you hate sport, make sure you go for a few long walks, or buy a bicycle and ride to college, or even go dancing.

Sleep

Last minute essays, revising for exams or a busy social life can all result in not getting enough sleep. Some people need more sleep than others, the average is about eight hours a night.

Drugs and alcohol

During your time as a student, you may possibly come across illegal drugs. You will almost certainly come across alcohol and you may be surprised at the extent to which some British students drink. Unless you are forbidden alcohol for religious or other reasons, drinking *small amounts* should not be a problem. If you are not used to drinking, however, large amounts of alcohol will definitely make you feel ill.

Some students amuse themselves by trying to out-drink each other, to see who can drink the most. If you find yourself in this kind of group, you do not have to join in, and you may feel that you would be better off changing the group you socialise with. Not all students are like this.

Just because you do not drink does not mean that you have to miss out! It is quite acceptable to go to a pub with friends and drink **soft drinks**, drinks with no alcohol content. In fact many people are now turning to low or non alcoholic drinks because of the very heavy restrictions on drinking and driving.

Drugs, on the other hand, *are* a problem because, apart from not being very good for you, they are also illegal. If you are caught using or possessing drugs you will almost certainly be deported.

There is absolutely nothing wrong with saying 'no' if you are offered alcohol or drugs.

There are several situations in which you may feel tempted to turn to either alcohol or drugs:

● because you are under stress and you feel they would help;
● because you are under pressure from other people to drink or to take drugs;
● because you feel that you will not fit in if you do not.

If you have a problem with either, there are several organisations which can help you. All advice is given in complete confidence.

— **Alcoholics Anonymous,** PO Box 1, Stonebow House, York YO1 2NJ. Tel: (0904) 644026 (for problems with drink);

— **Narcotics Anonymous,** PO Box 417, London SW10 ORS. Tel: (01) 351 6794 (for problems related to drugs).

You can find out where your nearest branch of these organisations is by going to a local Citizens Advice Bureau.

Finally, if you feel ill or have problems, whether they are with health, your studies or any personal problems, don't keep them to yourself;

● go to a doctor;
● go to the welfare officer at your college;
● talk to a teacher or lecturer.

If you do become ill and need to take time off college for any long periods of time, you must inform someone, otherwise you will be marked down as absent and you may have problems with the Home Office if they discover that you have been regularly missing classes (see Chapter 4).

9
Life as a Student — Work and Leisure

First day at college

Most schools and colleges have a **reception day** or a **registration day,** which is when all new students have to register their arrival at the college. Registration day is usually quite hectic. You will find yourself joining lots of queues and filling in a lot of forms. This is also the day when you will be given your lecture timetable.

If possible, try to arrive at the college a few days before registration day. This will give you time to settle in, get to know your surroundings and find out where everything is before the rush begins.

If you *are* planning to arrive at the college before registration day, and if you are staying in accommodation which has been provided or arranged by the college, tell them your arrival date so that they can make sure that the accommodation is ready for you.

STUDYING AND TEACHING METHODS

If you come from a country where the education system is very different from the British system, you may be faced with unfamiliar teaching and learning methods. Many students — including British students — are surprised by the difference between teaching methods in schools and those in further and higher education. In further and higher education:

● You are given much more time for studying on your own;

● You are not always dealing with facts, with right and wrong answers, any more. You are also going to be dealing with opinions, yours and other people's;

● Your tutor/lecturer is not there to give you all the facts you need, but there to help you to find the information for yourself and to form your own opinions on it;

● Teaching sessions may be more informal than you are used to.

While you are at college in Britain you will probably come across a variety of different teaching methods. The methods used will depend on the college and on the subject.

Lectures
In general this is when a **lecturer** stands at the front of a room full of students (you may find lectures being given to over a hundred people at one time, or just fifteen or twenty) and talks about a subject. The lecturer *may* invite questions or discussion at the end of the lecture.

● While you are at a lecture, take notes, *but don't try to write down everything the lecturer says.* You can't listen properly if you are writing all the time. Only write down essential information. Listen for expressions like *therefore, however, as a result, on the other hand, this proves that...* These are a signal that the lecturer is going to provide more information about a point he or she has just made.

● Before you go to a lecture, you should do some **background reading** on the subject. While you are reading, think of things you would like to find out, either from the lecture or from further reading.

● A lecture usually only contains a few **central ideas,** the rest will be an explanation of the ideas, the thinking behind the ideas and where these ideas might lead to. Reading about a subject before a lecture will inform you what those central ideas may be, and will give you key words to listen out for.

● If you *must* miss a lecture, make sure that you borrow a friend's notes, but don't think that you can use this method regularly and miss all your lectures. Other people's notes are not always easy to understand and are never the same as your own.

● Some lecturers will only give you a *taste* of a topic. Lectures are intended to guide you towards areas of further study. It will be up to you to read about the subject in more detail.

● Some lecturers, especially in science subjects, will be talking about their own research and will be giving you information which has not yet been published.

● After a lecture, don't go home and simply copy up your notes neatly and then forget about them. Combine them with the notes you make during your reading, make your own headings, put your notes into a form you can use. Some people, for example, like to rewrite their notes into the form of a diagram. Notes from this paragraph might end up looking like this:

Tutorials

A **tutorial** group will usually be a small group, of around five to ten students, sometimes even only one or two. Apart from that, a 'tutorial' could be any of the following, depending on the college:

● A discussion group where a topic is examined in great depth;

● A combination of lecture, questions and discussion;

● An opportunity for students to work on their own with the tutor available to answer questions;

● A session where a small group of students discuss their general work problems;

In some colleges, you will be given a **personal tutor.** This is someone who you arrange to see every week or every two weeks, at a set time, in order to discuss general problems you may be having with your work or with the college.

Seminars

The purpose of a seminar is for a small group of students to get together with a tutor for discussion and an exchange of ideas on a particular topic.

Often, some or all of the students in the group will have been asked to **prepare a paper** (write an essay) or solve a set of problems which they will present to the rest of the group at the seminar. The other students then discuss and criticise your paper or solutions. If you feel that your ideas are good, it is up to you to defend them. This will probably be a new (but very useful) experience for everyone and most people get very nervous about it.

Discussion groups provide the opportunity for students to share and exchange ideas, listen to other people's ideas and opinions, learn how to argue and how to accept criticism. One of the problems with discussion groups is that there always seems to be someone who does all the talking and others who don't say anything at all. Some people are not confident about speaking out in a group discussion, but a good tutor will lead everyone into the discussion.

As a student from overseas you may not feel confident that your English is good enough to join in the discussion. Try to join in, because people want to hear your ideas, not listen out for the grammatical mistakes you may be making.

Some tutorials can become lively intellectual debates...

Practicals
Some subjects require a great deal of **practical work** to be carried out. Most practical work will require preparation in advance and will have to be **written up** in a report when the work is finished.

Books
Although course textbooks are expensive everywhere, they are probably cheaper to buy in England than in your home country. You will also have the opportunity to buy **second-hand books,** some hardly ever used, from previous students.

When you receive your first reading list, don't rush off and buy all the books on it. You will find most of them in a library. Your teachers will advise you which books you should buy and which books you don't really need to buy. One book you *should* bring with you is a *bi-lingual dictionary,* your first language to English. Most book shops in Britain will only stock dictionaries in a few major languages.

Organising your time
When you get your timetable of lectures, tutorials and seminars from the college you will find that you have quite a lot of spare time available. This is the time you must organise into study periods and free periods.

If you do not organise your time, you will spend all your time on your favourite subjects and leave out the subjects which you dislike. Also time which you haven't organised will disappear very quickly — 'The essay isn't due to be given in for two weeks, there's plenty of time'. If you think like this, you may find yourself writing it the night before you have to hand it in. Make a **study timetable,** like the one opposite.

- Write in all your fixed activities, such as lectures, tutorials, meals.

- Decide how much free time you should give yourself each week.

- Divide the rest of the time between the different topics you are studying. If there is a topic you find more difficult than the others, give more time to this one.

- Give yourself time to do some background reading before lectures and time to review your notes after lectures.

- Try out your timetable for at least two weeks. If it doesn't work, don't abandon it, change it.

	MON	TUES	WED	THUR	FRI	SAT	SUN
9-10	LECTURE INTERNAT.	REVIEW NOTES	GENERAL READING	PRIVATE STUDIES STATS	LECTURE LABOUR ECONS.	FREE	FREE
10-11	ECONS.						
11-12	BREAK	SEMINAR	TUTORIAL	REVIEW NOTES	BREAK	FREE	FREE
12-1	PRIVATE STUDY ENGLISH		LECTURE ECON. PRINCS.		ENGLISH		
1-2	LUNCH	LUNCH		LUNCH	LUNCH	FREE	FREE
2-3	LECTURE ECON. RESEARCH	LECTURE STATS	BREAK	TUTORIAL	REVIEW NOTES OR		
3-4					GENERAL READING	PRIVATE STUDY	FREE
4-5	LECTURE ENGLISH	BREAK	SPORTS	PRIVATE STUDY	GENERAL READING	INT. ECONS.	
5-6		GENERAL READING		LABOUR ECONS			
6-7	DINNER	DINNER	DINNER	FREE	DINNER	FREE	GENERAL ASSIGNMENT
7-8	PREPARE / PREPARE	PREPARE FOR TUTORIAL	BREAK		FREE		WORK
8-9	SEMINAR		PREPARE FOR	FREE	PRIVATE STUDY	FREE	
9-10		PRIVATE STUDY	TUTORIAL		ECON. RESEARCH		
10-11		ECON. PRINCS					

Organising your time; a sample timetable for the week
might look like this.

- Don't let your timetable rule your life. If someone asks you to go out when it is one of your study periods, swap the study period for one of your free periods later on in the week.

- Don't take any notice of people who say they never do any work, that they haven't done the assignment, or that they haven't revised at all for the exams. For some reason most students don't like admitting that they ever do any work.

WHERE TO STUDY

It helps to find a favourite place where you can always go when you wish to study. This place should be warm and have plenty of natural light in the day-time and enough artificial light during the evening.

Some people prefer to work in their room at home, others can only work in a library. You might find that you like to change the place where you study if you get bored with sitting in the same place all the time. Coffee bars, pubs, trains or in front of a television are *not* ideal places to study.

A couple of good books available on how to study are:

— *Strengthening Your Study Skills: A guide for overseas students,* by Suzanne Salimbene. You can get it from The University of London Institute of Education, 20 Bedford Way, London WC1H OAL. Tel: (01) 636 1500.

— *Learn How to Study,* by D Rowntree, Macdonald Publishers, Greater London House, Hampstead Road, London NW1 7QX Tel: (01) 377 4600.

GETTING USED TO A NEW LIFE

Being away from home for the first time can cause problems for *any* student, but as a foreign student, you may have extra difficulties.

- In the space of just a few days you have to get used to a new school, a new home and a new country.
- You will be in a strange and unfamiliar environment.
- You will have to get used to unusual customs and different, often strange, ways of going about day-to-day life.
- Even simple things like obtaining money from a bank, catching a train, or using the telephone, can become major problems.
- You may be communicating in an unfamiliar language.
- You will be surrounded by people but there will be few, if any, familiar faces.

- People may not always be friendly.
- You cannot make a quick visit home whenever you feel lonely.
- Even phoning home may not be easy.

It's not surprising that many students become anxious and frustrated. You may also feel disappointed. You may have expected Britain to be very different to what you have actually found.

Things you may find disappointing

- Visitors to your home country may be treated as though they were valued guests. You may feel that you are not being given special treatment you had expected.

- The weather is cold and gloomy, but also damp. In winter, it becomes dark at around 4.30pm.

- Your English is not as good as you thought it was. In the classroom it was good, now no-one seems to understand you.

- The buildings seem ugly and monotonous. Unfortunately, the area around the railway station of any town, which is the part you will see first, is never very pleasant.

- People seem too busy to help you.

- Your first taste of British food may be in a station cafeteria. This is not a good example of British food.

- The accommodation you have been given is not what you had expected. It is probably not as big, as modern, as warm, or even as clean as you would have wanted.

- No-one seems to talk to you. Don't forget that the other students may be shy too.

- British students may seem to be much younger than you. They will also seem noisier, especially when they are in groups. You may think that they are not very serious about their studies.

Surviving disappointment

To avoid disappointment, try to read as much about Britain as possible before you come. Also talk to people who have been to Britain as students. Don't let them tell you that life was wonderful. Ask them to tell you about the problems they had and the disappointments they experienced.

Even when you have lived in Britain for some time, there will still be things which surprise you, strange customs which you don't know about, times when you feel you have made a fool of yourself because you didn't know what to do or what to say.

Studies show that there is a pattern to settling into a new environment. If you know in advance, how you are going to feel, you may find it easier to cope.

People tend to go through the following stages:

Stage One, initial excitement. Everything is new and interesting.

Stage Two, initial culture shock. A few things start to go wrong. Differences between your own culture and the new culture start to cause problems. What was once new and exciting now seems unfamiliar and frustrating.

Stage Three, you begin to get used to it.

Stage Four, you thought you had got used to it, but one or two minor things go wrong and it feels as if the whole world is against you. Some people give up at this stage, or become aggressive or withdrawn.

Stage Five, adjustment. You either integrate into the new culture, or decide that you don't like it but have to tolerate it for now.

Feeling at home in Britain
If everything around you is strange and unfamiliar, you can feel isolated and insecure.

When you were at home you were in a village, town or city which was familiar. You knew where everything was and how to get there, you knew the shops, some of the faces in the streets, you may have had a favourite bar or restaurant. You could recognise labels on the goods in shops, and you knew what you were buying instead of being faced with a disappointment when you opened the tin or packet. The clothes you wore were more or less the same as those worn by everyone else. Now all this has been replaced by foreign and unfamiliar things.

The following steps will help you to feel at home in your new environment, and it is surprising what a difference they will make. Soon you will begin to feel more confident and secure.

● You will probably only have one room. Make this room your home. Put pictures on the walls and buy a few small things to add a personal touch. Bring some things with you from home, so you have something familiar around you.

- Explore your immediate environment. Go to your local shops, walk round the nearby streets and make them familiar to you. See what there is in your area. You may discover a park, a museum, a theatre, a sports centre or a friendly cafe, just round the corner.

- Pluck up courage to talk to local shop keepers and neighbours. It will be a while before they recognise you and say 'hello' first, but it *will* happen. If you are living in college accommodation your neighbours will be other students, which will make it easier.

- Locate the local library, post office, police station, hospital, welfare office and so on, so you will know where they are when you need them.

- Find out where you can buy food from your home country. Find out if there is a local restaurant which serves your national dishes.

- Locate any other students who come from your country. If, before you leave home, you know of anyone living in the town, contact them before you leave. You probably don't want to spend all your time in Britain with people from your home country, but it helps to have the contact. If you know that you are not completely alone, and that there are other people who may have the same problems, it will help to talk to them.

- Try to join in plenty of social events organised by your college. At first no-one will know anyone else, so you will all be looking for new friends

- If your college does not arrange social events, find out where other students go in the evenings.

- Join a club — for example, a sports club, or a dancing society. Join in as many things as you can. If your college does not have any, get information about local clubs in your area from the local library.

- Talk to British people. Ask questions. People love to show off what they know and some people actually like helping out.

- If you are rejected, try again. This is probably the hardest thing to do.

After you have got used to living in Britain, and you return to your home country, everything there will feel strange and unfamiliar. You may have to go through the same process all over again!

DOs and DON'Ts in case of depression

● Don't isolate yourself. This will make your problems worse in the end because you will get lonely.

● Don't be hostile to British students because you are unhappy.

● Don't spend all your time with a small group of students from overseas, and ignoring British students. Try to make British friends as well — they might be able to explain the things about British life which you find strange.

● Don't be afraid to ask questions.

● Make full use of the organisations which are there to help students and visitors from overseas (see Appendix 2).

● Don't think that socialising is a waste of time. You cannot spend all your time studying. It is very important to relax as well. You will also find that while students are eating and drinking and talking together, they are often discussing their last lecture or their next assignment, or exchanging valuable opinions and ideas on each other's work.

IF YOU GET LONELY

Many colleges organise events and make special arrangements for overseas students to help them to avoid becoming lonely and isolated. Make full use of such schemes. If your college does not do anything like this you should look for similar things in the local community. Your local library will be a good source of information on what is available.

The following are a few of the schemes and activities which you will probably find.

Fresher's week

In many colleges, an event called **Fresher's week,** sometimes called **Intro week** or **Fresher's fair,** usually takes place during the first week of term. The week usually includes a programme of social events and some more formal lectures and meetings, all intended to help you become familiar with the college and its environment and to find out what the entertainment and social life is like. Fresher's week also gives you a great opportunity to meet people and make new friends.

Some of the activities you might expect to find during Fresher's week include:

- discos and dances;
- cheese and wine parties;
- concerts;
- a brief talk by the Vice Chancellor or Principal, followed by drinks;
- an opportunity to join one or several of the college's clubs or societies;
- lectures by people from the local community on life in London/Manchester/Cambridge....or wherever you are.

During this week, you will be bombarded with information, leaflets, introductions, people saying, 'If you have any problems, do come and see me.' Do not worry of you can't remember everything, or if you don't remember anyone's name. You can always find out later. Some colleges also have an Intro event especially for the students from overseas, often called an **Induction course** or **Orientation course.** This will usually take place *before* the main Intro week.

A TYPICAL TWO-DAY ORIENTATION COURSE ORGANISED BY A UNIVERSITY

Sunday September 24th		4.30-5	An overseas student talks about life in Britain
2pm-6pm	Students arrive and settle into accommodation		
6.30pm	Welcome by the Vice Chancellor Dinner	5-6	Video, the university and the town.
Monday September 25th		7.30	Dinner, folk dancing
9-10	Introductory meeting		
10-10.30	Coffee	**Tuesday September 26th**	
10.30-11.30	A talk on the British educational system	10-12	English language tests
11.30-1pm	How to use the library, visit and talk	12-12.30	Student accommodation
1-2.30	Lunch	12.30-5	Lunch and coach tour to local places of interest
2.30-4.30	An information session on: the Home Office, health, money, welfare.	7pm	Dinner

Peer pairing scheme

At the moment, only a few colleges run **peer pairing schemes,** but the idea is becoming more and more popular. The scheme depends on the support of existing students, who volunteer to take part.

Each new student from overseas who enrols at the college is **paired** with a student who is already studying at the college. The students might write to each other before the new student arrives in the country, otherwise the two students meet during the first few days of term.

The existing student agrees to contact the new student once or twice each week, so he or she can make sure that the new student is not experiencing any problems, and, if so, can either help out or advise where to go for help. The student union will be able to tell you if such a scheme operates in your college.

Hospitality schemes

During the Christmas vacation, most British students go home to their families, and most facilities, including shops, close down for several days. This can be a difficult time for students from overseas. You may decide to stay in Britain for a number of reasons. For example, perhaps you can't afford to travel home for this short vacation, especially if your sponsor only pays for one return trip per year.

There are two organisations which can arrange for you to go to stay with a British family during the Christmas, and also Easter and summer, vacations, and at weekends throughout the year.

- **Hosting for Overseas Students,** 18 Northumberland Avenue, London WC2N 5AP. Tel: (01) 925 2595. Their family stays are free of charge.
- **Experiment in International Living,** Upper Wyche, Malvern, Worcestershire WR14 4EN. Tel: (06845) 62577.

FEMALE STUDENTS AND WIVES OF STUDENTS

As well as the usual problems which students from overseas experience, women may find that they have some extra adjustments to make.

Different countries see women in different roles, and different cultures dictate different ways of behaviour. You may find that life for women in Britain is very different from life for women in your own country. Some are surprised at the amount of freedom and independence women seem to have in Britain. Others may be used to women having a higher status and more freedom than in some societies within Britain.

As the wife of a student, and not a student yourself, you may find adjustment much more difficult. You might feel isolated because you:

- are not part of a ready-made student community;

- are alone in the home all day, especially if you are looking after small children;
- can't speak English very well.

Some colleges do provide facilities, including English lessons, especially for the wives of overseas students.

THE STUDENT UNION

All universities, polytechnics and some of the larger colleges have a **student union**. Every student at the college is automatically a member.

If your college does not have its own student union, you can join the **National Union of Students** by writing to NUS, Nelson Mandela House, 461 Holloway Road, London N7 6LJ. Tel: (01) 272 8900.

A college student union provides a variety of very useful services to its members. Usually it:

- Organises student clubs and societies.
- Organises social activities and sporting activities.
- Offers advice and practical help for students with problems of any kind.
- Provides information about cheap travel, insurance, and other benefits which are available to students.
- Is a source of information about local events.
- May run a 'niteline', a phone line for people with personal problems.
- May run an accommodation office.

If your college does not have its own student union, you will be able to join in activities and use facilities run by the student union at a larger college nearby.

Social life and entertainment

Facilities for entertainment depend a great deal on where you are living. Some towns, for example, may have only one cinema, but London has hundreds. The best place to find out about entertainment in your area is a **local newspaper** or a tourist information centre. Some cities have their own entertainment listings magazine. London, for example has *Time Out* and *What's on in London*.

Don't forget that if you have a student card, you may be able to get a discount on prices at many cinemas, theatres, concerts and some restaurants. But entertainment in the outside world will always be more expensive than that provided by your college.

Pubs

Much of a student's social life centres upon pubs and wine bars.

Each one has a different style and atmosphere. Some are quiet and traditional, others modern and noisy, Some have discos, and many have games such as darts, snooker or pool. The main thing to remember is that *you do not have to drink alcohol* just because you are in a pub. Pubs are also places where people go to relax and be with friends.

Many pubs in Britain now open all day (11am to 11pm Monday to Saturday and 12.30pm to 2.30pm, 7pm to 10.30pm on Sunday). When it is near to closing time, you will hear a bell ring or someone shouting 'Last orders, please!'

As well as serving drinks, many pubs serve food and, especially in the countryside, they are the best places to get a good, inexpensive, British lunch or evening meal.

Many people in pubs drink **beer**. Note that the beer in England is not much like beer back home. If you want something similar to the beer you may be used to, ask for **lager**. When you go to a pub with a group of people, each person usually **buys a round** (a drink for everyone in your group).

Eating out
Although eating out is not always good value for money, it can make a change to home cooking or college food. In large towns and cities, there are restaurants which serve food from many different countries, as well as different types of traditional British food.

Fast food/take-aways
A take-away meal is a meal which you can buy already cooked, so that you can carry it home and eat it immediately. The traditional British fast take-away food is fish and chips. A portion of fish and chips is very filling, quite nutritious and will not cost much more than £1.50. Most towns have American style Hamburger restaurants, pizza bars and Greek, Chinese and Indian take-aways. Another popular form of take-away snack is a sandwich from a **sandwich bar.**

Restaurants
There are so many different restaurants, of different qualities and prices, that it is difficult to generalise. Most display a menu outside the door so that you can see what they serve and how much you have to pay, before you go in. Beware of those which don't, they are usually expensive.

When you pay, it is normal to add an extra 10% for service. This is *sometimes* already included on the bill, so watch out for it. If it is not, most people leave the extra money, in cash, on the table for the waiter or waitress to pick up. This is called a 'tip'.

Concerts

In Britain, most musical tastes are catered for, from classical music and jazz to folk music and rock. Details of pop, rock and jazz concerts can be found in national music papers like *New Musical Express* and *Melody Maker,* which you can buy from most large newsagents.

For classical music and opera, get details from the local tourist information centre or from a national newspaper.

Theatres

Again, the best places to find details of what is on at your local theatre are the tourist information centre, and national and local newspaper. A popular, and usually cheaper, form of theatre is something called **fringe theatre.** Fringe theatre companies perform in smaller theatres and sometimes in pubs and bars.

For theatre performances in larger towns, you usually have to book tickets some time before the performance, although if you want to take a risk, you can go to a theatre just before the time of the performance and get cheap **standby tickets.** In London, there is a half-price theatre ticket office in Leicester Square. You can go there between 2.30 and 6.30pm on the day of the performance to get cheap tickets for a variety of different shows.

RELIGION

The two main religions practised in Britain are **Church of England (Protestant)** and **Catholic.** However, most of the major world religions are represented in Britain. You can get information about local facilities from the centres listed below, or from your *Yellow Pages* telephone directory.

Anglican Chaplaincy to the
Universities in London,
Church of Christ the King,
Gordon Square,
London WC1H OAG.
Tel: (01) 387 0670.

The Buddhist Society,
58 Eccleston Square,
London SW1V 1PH.
Tel: (01) 834 5858.

The Baptist Union of Great
Britain and Ireland,
4 Southampton Row,
London WC1B 4AB.
Tel: (01) 405 9803.

Catholic International
Students Centre,
41 Holland Park,
London W11 3RP.
Tel: (01) 727 3047.

Church of Scotland,
121 George Street,
Edinburgh EH2 4YN.
Tel: (031) 225 5722.

Churches Commission on
Overseas Students,
1 Stockwell Green,
London SW9 9HP,
Tel: (01) 737 1101.

Ghanaian Chaplaincy Office,
Whitfield Memorial,
American Church,
79 Tottenham Court Road,
London W1P 9HA.
Tel: (01) 580 6433.

Hindu Centre,
39 Grafton Terrace,
London NW5 4JA.
Tel: (01) 485 8200.

Islamic Centre,
146 Park Road,
London NW8 7RG.
Tel: (01) 724 3363.

Methodist Church Overseas Mission,
25 Marylebone Road,
London NW1 5JR.
Tel: (01) 935 2541.

Quaker International Centre,
1 Byng Place,
London WC1E 7JH.
Tel: (01) 387 5648.

Spanish Catholic Chaplaincy,
47 Palace Court,
London W2 4LS.
Tel: (01) 229 8815.

UK Turkish Islamic Cultural Centre,
5 Hayling Close,
London N16 8UR.
Tel: (01) 254 0373.

Chinese Overseas Christian
Mission,
4 Earlsfield Road,
London SW18 3DW.
Tel: (01) 870 2251.

Federal Student Islamic
Society,
38 Mapesbury Road,
London NW2 4JD.
Tel: (01) 452 4493.

Hillel House,
B'nai Brith Foundation,
1-2 Endsleigh Street,
London WC1H ODS.
Tel: (01) 388 0801.

International Lutheran Student
Centre,
30 Thanet Street,
London WC1J 9QH.
Tel: (01) 388 4848.

London Baha'I Centre,
27 Rutland Gate
London SW7 1PD.
Tel: (01) 584 0843.

Muslim Information Service,
233 Seven Sisters Road,
London N4 4DA.
Tel: (01) 272 5170.

Sikh Temple,
62 Queensdale Road,
London W11 4SG.
Tel: (01) 603 2789.

UK Islamic Mission,
202 North Gower Street,
London NW1 2LY.
Tel: (01) 387 2157.

GETTING A JOB

If you are in Britain as a student, don't expect to be able to work to help pay for your course or your living expenses, because:

- You may not be able to obtain a part-time work permit;
- If you have permission to enter Britain as a full-time student, you will not be allowed to work full-time;
- You will not have time to work *and* concentrate on your studies;
- You may not be able to get a job. Jobs are not easy to find in Britain.

However, many students do want work during the vacation, at weekends or as a necessary part of their course.

Work permits

British citizens and **citizens of EC countries** do *not* need to obtain permission to work. Anyone else who wishes to take a full-time or part-time job in Britain *must* obtain a work permit.

Do not take a job if you have not been given a work permit. If the authorities discover that you are working without a permit, you could face a fine or a prison sentence. You would certainly not be allowed to extend your leave to remain in Britain in order to complete your studies.

Who can apply for a work permit?

If you are thinking of finding work, first of all check that you are eligible to apply for a work permit. Look at the stamp you were given in your passport when you entered Britain.

Before you apply for *any* type of work permit it is very important that you get advice from either;

- someone at your college;
- UKCOSA (see Appendix 2);
- your student union.

If you apply for permission to work when you are not eligible to do so, you could cause yourself problems when you apply for permission to remain in Britain (see Chapter 4).

What type of work can you obtain?

The following are the *only* types of work for which you can obtain permission:

- part-time work

Can you apply for a work permit?

Leave to enter the United Kingdom, on condition that the holder does not enter or change employment paid or unpaid without the consent of the Secretary of State for Employment, and does not engage in any business or profession without the consent of the Secretary of State for the Home Department, is hereby given for/until

....


```
INMIGRATION OFFICER
*   (790)   *
2 7 NOV 1979
HEATHROW (3)
```

The holder is also required to register at once with the police.

This means that you have a restriction on being able to work. It means that you may apply for a work permit.

Leave to enter the United Kingdom, on condition that the holder does not enter employment paid or unpaid and does not engage in any business or profession, is hereby given for/until

....


```
INMIGRATION OFFICER
*   (790)   *
2 7 NOV 1979
HEATHROW (3)
```

This means that you are prohibited from working. You cannot apply for permission to take any kind of work. You can apply for permission to have this stamp changed, but do not do this without obtaining advice from UKCOSA (see appendix 2).

Leave to enter the United Kingdom is hereby given for/until

....


```
INMIGRATION OFFICER
*   (790)   *
2 7 NOV 1979
HEATHROW (3)
```

This means that you can work and that you do not need to obtain permission to work.

- vacation work
- practical training at the end of your course
- practical work experience during your course
- work as a post graduate research assistant
- nursing
- work as a doctor or dentist
- work as an au pair

Part-time work and vacation work

Many students look for work during the long summer vacation, and some take **part-time** jobs in the evenings or at weekends. If you want to take a part-time job you must apply for a permit *each time* you take a different job.

In order to obtain permission you must:

1. Find a job.
2. Go to a local **Department of Employment** office (address in telephone directory) or to a **Jobcentre,** and ask for **form OW1 and leaflet OW5.**
3. Give form OW1 to your employer and ask him to complete it.
4. Take the form back to the Department of Employment or Jobcentre, with:
   - your passport;
   - your police registration certificate,
   - a letter from your school or college which states that taking the job will not, in their opinion, disrupt your studies.

Practical training during your course

On some courses, which are called **sandwich courses,** students spend some time gaining skills or practical work experience as part of their course. On other courses you may have to work and gain practical experience during your long vacation. Some colleges make the application for a work permit for all students on the course. You should find out if your college does this before you apply for yourself. If you do need to make your own application:

1. Write to **The Under Secretary of State,** Department of Employment, Ebury Bridge House, Ebury Bridge Road, London SW1, asking for general approval to take up training/employment which is an obligatory part of your course.

2. Enclose a letter from your college which states:

- your full name, address, date of birth
- passport details
- details of the course you are taking
- length of the course
- details of training required by the course.

3. Wait for the reply, which will be sent to the college.

Once you have been given permission to take work as a necessary part of your course, you can change jobs as often as you need to, without re-applying for permission, but *only while you are enrolled on the course*. Once your course has ended, don't work without reapplying for permission. If you want to take part-time or vacation work which is *not* related to your course, you must obtain separate permission, as described on page 183.

Some students on sandwich courses do have difficulty in trying to find work. *Before* you enroll on a course of this kind, check whether the college can *guarantee* to find you work.

Practical training at the end of your course

At the end of your course, you may need to gain some practical experience or training in an area related to the course you have just taken. You *may* be given permission to take this type of work, if you can satisfy the Department of Employment that:

- you would *not* be able to receive such training in your home country;
- you intend to return to your home country when you have completed the training;

In order to obtain permission you must:

1. Find a job.
2. Go to a local **Department of Employment office** or **Jobcentre** and obtain form **OW22** plus leaflet **OW21.**
3. Give the form OW22 to your employer and ask him to complete it.
4. Return the form to the address shown on the form.

Once you have been given permission to take a particular job, you cannot change your employment without going through the same process again.

Postgraduate research assistant

A university might want to employ you as a research assistant, or you may need to take up a paid post as a research assistant in order to gain a PhD. In either of these cases, the *university* must apply to the Department of Employment, for permission to give you this employment.

You can obtain further information about getting permission to work as a research assistant from **The Committee of Vice Chancellors and Principals,** 29 Tavistock Square, London WC1. Tel: (01) 387 9231.

Nursing

If you have completed a course of nursing training at a hospital in Britain, you can apply for permission to work as a nurse or a midwife. You can obtain further details from **The Royal College of Nursing,** 20 Cavendish Square, London W1M OAB. Tel: (01) 409 3333.

Doctors and dentists

If you are a doctor or a dentist, and you are registered with The General Medical Council, you can apply for permission to gain practical training in a hospital. You can obtain details from **The Overseas Registration Division,** 153 Cleveland Street, London W1. Tel: (01) 387 2556.

You will be given permission to stay in Britain for a period of one year. If you want to stay longer, you have to re-apply every twelve months. The maximum length of time you can stay for this purpose is four years.

Au pairs

Certain categories of people can come to Britain to combine studying English language with work as an **au pair** for an English speaking family. You can come to Britain as an au pair if:

- you are female;
- you are single;
- you are between the ages of 17 and 27;
- you are from a western European country.

While you are an au pair, you may not take any other type of employment.

Au pairs are allowed to remain in Britain for a **maximum** of two years. You can obtain further information about working as an au pair from; **The Federation of Recruitment and Employment Services,** 10 Belgrave Square, London SW1X 8PH. Tel: (01) 235 6616.

Other types of full-time work, and work as a self-employed person

Anyone (except EC nationals) who wants to come to Britain to take full-time employment, or to set themselves up as a self-employed person, must apply for permission to do so *before coming to Britain.* You cannot enter Britain as a student and then apply for permission to work once you are here. Ask the **British High Commission** or **Embassy** in your home country for details on how to apply.

DEPENDANTS AND WORK

Dependants, wives and children over 18, of a male who has come to Britain as a student, are allowed to work without permission, *if the husband/father has a restriction on work stamped in his passport.*

If the husband/father has a *prohibition* on taking work, then the wife or child *cannot* work unless the prohibition has been taken away.

10
Going Home

As soon as you have settled down and become used to living in Britain, it will be time to return to your home country again. Many people find that adjusting to their home country — its customs, society and attitudes — causes the same problems they encountered when they first came to Britain. Going home can lead to culture shock in reverse! For example:

● Old friends, and even some relatives may now seem like strangers.

● Your home town, or the house you lived in, may not be the same as you remembered it. Memory is selective and you may be disappointed by the reality.

● While you were in Britain, your attitudes, opinions and behaviour probably changed. Perhaps they are very different now from those of the people back home.

● Life at home may seem slow and quiet compared with the hectic life of a college student.

● You may not have as much freedom as you experienced as a student.

● Life in your home country may have changed since you were there. Maybe there has been a change of government, or your own political views have changed.

● The education you received while you were at college may now seem irrelevant to the life you must now lead.

● You may not be able to get a job.

● You have had to leave new friends you made while you were at college.

You can avoid some of these things by:

● keeping in touch with your friends and family while you are in Britain;

● regularly reading newspapers from your home country;

● preparing yourself for your return home by thinking of all the positive aspects which you missed while you were away;

● keeping in touch with your college friends when you return home.

Baggage

You will probably have more luggage to take home than you brought with you. If you are travelling by land and sea, you can take as much as you like — but don't forget you will have to carry it! If you are travelling by plane, you may have to pay excess baggage, which can be expensive. The agency or airline where you buy your ticket will tell you your baggage allowance (usually 15-20 kgs). If you have more, consider shipping it in advance or sending it by **unaccompanied air freight**. Details are available from the airline or any travel agent.

Finally

Going to live in a new environment might be a difficult experience, but it is also a challenging and very rewarding one. Hopefully the good times will outnumber the bad. Remember that when you leave, you will be able to take home the qualifications you have gained — and, just as important, many happy memories and lasting friendships as well.

USEFUL CHECKLISTS

Ready to go?
Make sure you have received a letter of unconditional acceptance from your school or college. ☐

Obtain a scholarship, or enough money to pay for your fees and living expenses. Obtain proof of these. ☐

Obtain entry clearance from the British Embassy or High Commission in your home country. ☐

Arrange foreign exchange. ☐

Arrange for regular payments of money to be paid from your bank to a bank in England. ☐

Arrange accommodation, even if only temporary. ☐

Calculate how much money you will need to travel from your port of entry to your final destination, plus money for your journey and money for your first few days in Britain. Order travellers cheques and British currency. ☐

Buy travel tickets and travel insurance. ☐

Check your baggage allowance (usually 15-20kgs). ☐

Check whether you will be covered by the NHS while you are in Britain. If not, take out a medical insurance policy. ☐

Check whether you need a medical certificate for entry into Britain. ☐

If you are currently using any drugs or medicines which have been prescribed by your doctor, obtain a letter of explanation from the doctor. ☐

Buy an International Student Identity card. ☐

Ask the college for the telephone number of someone you can contact, in case you have any problems on your journey. ☐

Label all your luggage with your name, your address in Britain and the address of the college you will be attending. ☐

Plan your journey from your port of entry into Britain, to your final destination. Find out the names of stations or airports you need to get to, and work out how you will get there. Write the names down, in case you need to ask someone for help. If possible, find out the times of all the connecting planes/trains you will need to catch. ☐

Take some passport-sized photographs of yourself. ☐

Documents you will need on your journey

Make sure that you carry the following things with you, and do not pack them in your luggage.

Tickets

Passport, with visa/letter of consent/entry certificate.

Letter of acceptance from a school or college.

Address of your final destination.

Telephone number of your school or college, or of someone you can contact in case you have any problems.

Recent bank statements/sponsor's letter/proof of scholarship.

Insurance documents.

Medical certificate (if required).

Four small photographs of yourself (you will need all of these within a few days of arriving in Britain).

At your destination — a checklist

Check into your accommodation.

Phone home.

Register with the police.

If you sent money over in advance, check that it has arrived.

Open a bank account.

Register your arrival at the college.

Obtain a programme of events for new students

Collect your timetable and reading list.

Join the student union, if there is one.

Check whether you are entitled to NHS treatment. If not, take out a medical insurance policy, if you did not obtain one in your home country.

Register with a doctor.

Take out any other insurance policies you may need (car, personal belongings).

Conversion tables for weights and measures

Length

1 inch (in)	= 2.54 centimetres (cm)	1 centimetre	= 0.394 inches
1 foot (ft)	= 30.48 centimetres	1 metre	= 3 feet, 3 inches
1 yard (yd)	= 0.91 metres (m)	1 kilometre	= 0.621 miles
1 mile (m)	= 1.61 kilometres (km)		

Weight

1 ounce (oz)	= 28.35 grams	1 kilogram	= 2 pounds, 3 ounces
1 pound (lb)	= 0.45 kilograms (kg)	1 tonne	= 0.984 UK tons
1 stone (st)	= 6.3 kilograms		
1 UK ton	= 1.016 tonnes		

Volume

1 pin (pt)	= 0.57 litres	1 litre	= 1.75 pints
1 gallon	= 4.55 litres		

Appendix 1
British Council Offices
Worldwide

Offices in Britain

London: 10 Spring Gardens, London SW1A 2BN. Tel: (01) 930 8466.

Belfast: 1 Chlorine Gardens, Belfast BT9 5DJ. Tel: (0232) 666706.

Birmingham: 2nd Floor, Burnley House, 13 Temple Street, Birmingham B2 5BN. Tel: (021) 632 5482.

Brighton: First Floor, London Gate, 72 Dyke Road Drive, Brighton, East Sussex BN1 6AJ. Tel: (0273) 542411.

Bristol: 7 Priory Road, Tyndall's Park Road, Bristol BS8 1UA. Tel: (0272) 738466.

Cambridge: Bishop Bateman Court, 5/7 New Park Street, Cambridge CB5 8AT. Tel: (0223) 354786.

Cardiff: 28 Park Place, Cardiff CF1 3QE. Tel: (0222) 397346.

Dundee: 8 Perth Road, Dundee DD1 4LN. Tel: (0382) 21978.

Edinburgh: 3 Bruntsfield Crescent, Edinburgh EH10 4HD. Tel: (031) 447 4716.

Glasgow: 6 Belmont Crescent, Glasgow G12 8ES. Tel: (041) 339 8651.

Hull: 138 Cottingham Road, Hull HU6 7RY. Tel: (0482) 43265.

Leeds: 1 St. Mark's Avenue, Leeds LS2 9BJ. Tel: (0532) 445211.

Leicester: 259 London Road, Leicester LE2 3BE. Tel: (0533) 706574.

Manchester: 139 Barlow Moor Road, West Didsbury, Manchester M20 8PS. Tel: (061) 434 4311.

Newcastle: 89/91 Jesmond Road, Newcastle upon Tyne NE2 1PF. Tel: (091) 281 4366.

Nottingham: 8 Sherwood Rise, Nottingham NG7 6JF. Tel: (0602) 621939.

Oxford: 1 Beaumont Place, Oxford OX1 2PJ. Tel: (0865) 572236.

Sheffield: 305 Glossop Road, Sheffield S10 2HL. Tel: (0742) 754822.

Swansea: Fulton House, University College Swansea, Singleton Park, Swansea SA2 8PP. Tel: (0792) 297713.

OVERSEAS OFFICES

Algeria: 6 Avenue Souidani Boudjemaa, Algiers. Tel: 60 55 22.

Australia: Edgecliff Centre, 203/233 New South Head Road, PO Box 88, Edgecliff NSW 2027. Tel: 326 2022.

Austria: Schenkenstrasse 4, A-1010 Vienna. Tel: 533 26 16.

Bahrain: 21 Government Avenue, PO Box 452, Manama 306. Tel: 251415.

Bangladesh: 5 Fuller Road, PO Box 161, Dhaka 2, Tel: 500107.

Belgium & Luxembourg: Britannia House, rue Joseph II/Joseph II Straat 30, 1040 Brussels. Tel: 219 36 00.

Botswana: British High Commission Building, Queens Road, The Mall, PO Box 439, Gaborone. Tel: 353602.

Brazil: SCRN 708/9-BLF Nos 1/3, Caixa Postal 6104, 70.740 Brasilia DF. Tel: 272 3060.

Brunei: PO Box 3049, Room 45, 5th Floor, Hong Kong Bank Chambers, Jalan Pemancha, Bandar Seri Begawan. Tel: 27531.

Bulgaria: British Embassy, Boulevard Marshal, Tolbukhin 65-67, Sofia. Tel: 885361.

Burma: British Embassy, 80 Strand Road, PO Box 638, Rangoon. Tel: 81700.

Cameroon: Les Galéries, avenue J F Kennedy, BP 818, Yaoundé. Tel: 22 31 72.

Canada: British High Commission, 80 Elgin Street, Ottawa, Ontario K1P 5K7. Tel: 237 1530.

Chile: Eliodoro Yañez 832, Casilla 15-T Tajamar, Santiago, Tel: 2234622.

China: British Embassy, 11 Guang Hua Lu, Jian Guo Men Wai, Beijing. Tel: 532 1961. 244 Yong Fu Lu, Shanghai. Tel: 374569.

Colombia: Calle 87 No 12-79, Apartado Aéreo 089231, Bogotá 1. Tel: 257 9632.

Côte d'Ivoire: British Embassy Immeuble, Angle Boulevard Card et avenue Dr Jamot Plateau, Abidjan. Tel: 22 68 50.

Cyprus: 3 Museum Street, PO Box 5654, Nicosia, Tel: 442152.

Czechoslovakia: British Embassy, Jungmannova 30, 110 00 Prague 1. Tel: 22 4501.

Denmark: Møntergade 1, 1116 Copenhagen K. Tel: 11 20 44.

East-Jerusalem: 31 Nablus Road, PO Box 19136, Jerusalem. Tel: 282545.

Ecuador: Av. Amazonas 1646, Casilla 8829, Quito. Tel: 520 653.

Egypt: 192 Sharia el Nil, Agouza, Cairo. Tel: 3453281.

Ethiopia: Artistic Building, Adwa Avenue, PO Box 1043, Addis

Ababa. Tel: 11 00 22.

Finland: Erottajankatu 7B, 00130 Helsinki 13. Tel: 640505.

Fiji: British Development Division in the South Pacific, Private Mailbag Suva, Vanua House, Victoria Parade, Suva, Fiji. Tel: 301744.

France: 9 rue de Constantine, 75007 Paris. Tel: 45 55 95 95.

German Democratic Republic: British Embassy, Unter den Linden 32/34, East Berlin BFPO 45, Berlin 108. Tel: 220 2431.

Federal Republic of Germany: Hahnenstrasse 6, 5000 Köln 1. Tel: 23 66 77. Rothenbaumchaussee 34, 2000 Hamburg 13. Tel: 44 60 57.

Ghana: Liberia Road, Accra. Tel: 221766.

Greece; Etairias 17, Kolanaki Square, Athens 106 73, PO Box 3488, 102 10 Athens. Tel: 3633211. Ethnikis Amynis 9, PO Box 10289, 541 10 Salonica. Tel: 235 236.

Hong Kong: Easey Commercial Building, 255 Hennessy Road, Wanchai, Hong Kong. Tel: 831 5138.

Hungary: Harmincad Utca 6, Budapest V. Tel: 182 888.

India: British High Commission, British Council Division, AIFACS Building, Rafi Marg, New Delhi 110/001. Tel: 381401. British Deputy High Commission, Mittal Tower, C Wing, Nariman Point, Bombay 400 021. Tel: 223560. British Deputy High Commission, 5 Shakespeare Sarani, Calcutta 700071. Tel: 445378.

Indonesia: S Widjojo Centre, Jalan Jendral Sudirman 71, Jakarta, Tel: 587411.

Iraq: Waziriya 301, Street 3, Houses 22 and 24, PO Box 298, Baghdad, Tel: 4220091.

Israel: 140 Hayarkon Street, PO Box 3302, Tel Aviv 61032. Tel: 222 194.

Italy: Palazzo del Drago, Via Quattro Fontane 20, 00184 Rome. Tel: 4756641.

Japan: 2-Kagurazaka 1-Chome, Shinjuku-ku, Tokyo 162. Tel: 2358031.

Jordan: Rainbow Street, Jabal Amman, PO Box 634, Amman. Tel: 63147.

Kenya: ICEA Building, Kenyatta Avenue, PO Box 40751, Nairobi. Tel: 334855.

Korea: 4th floor, Anglican Church Annexe, 3/7 Chung Dong, Choong-ku, Seoul. Tel: 737 7157.

Kuwait: 2 al Arabi Street, PO Box 345, Mansouriyah. Tel: 2533204.

Lesotho: Hobsons Square, PO Box 429, Maseru 100. Tel: 312609.

Malawi: Plot 13/20, City Centre, PO Box 30222, Lilongwe 3, Tel: 730266.

Malaysia: Jalan Bukit Aman 50480, Kuala Lumpur 10-01, PO Box 10539, Peninsular Malaysia. Tel: 2987555. First floor, Bangunan Ang Cheng Ho, Jalan Tunku Abdul Rahman, PO Box 615, Sarawak, East Malaysia. Tel: 56271.

Mauritius: Royal Road, PO Box 111, Rose Hill. Tel: 541601.

Mexico: Maestro Antonio Caso 127, Col. San Rafael, Apdo Postal 30-588, Mexico City 06470 DF. Tel: 566 61 44.

Morocco: 22 avenue Moulay Youssef, BP 427, Rabat. Tel: 608 36.

Nepal: Kantipath, PO Box 640, Kathmandu. Tel: 221305.

Netherlands: Keizersgracht 343, 1016 EH Amsterdam. Tel: 22 36 44.

New Zealand: Reserve Bank Building, 2 The Terrace, PO Box 1812, Wellington 1. Tel: 726 049.

Nigeria: 11 Kingsway Royal, Ikoyi, PO Box 3702, Lagos, Tel: 610210. Hospital Road, PO Box 81, Kanduna, Tel: 243484.

Norway: Fridtjof Nansens Plass 5, 0160 Oslo 1. Tel: 42 68 48.

Oman: Road One, Medinat Qaboos West, PO Box 7090 Jibroo. Tel: 600548.

Pakistan: 23 87th Street G 6/3, PO Box 1135, Islamabad. Tel: 822504. 20 Bleak House Road, PO Box 10410, Karachi 0406. Tel: 512036.

Peru: Calle Alberto Lynch, San Isidro, Lima 14. Tel: 70 43 50.

Philippines: 7, 3rd Street, New Manila, PO Box AC168, Cubao, Quezon City, Metro Manila. Tel: 7211981.

Poland: Al Jerozolimskie 59, 00-678 Warsaw. Tel: 287401.

Portugal: Rua Cecilio De Sousa 65, 1294 Lisbon Codex. Tel: 369208.

Qatar: Ras Abu Aboud Road, PO Box 2992, Doha. Tel: 426193.

Romania: British Embassy, 24 Strada Jules Michelet, Bucharest. Tel: 111634.

Saudi Arabia: Dabab Street, PO Box 2701, Mura'aba, Riyadh 11461. Tel: 402 1650.

Senegal: British Embassy, 20 rue du Docteur Guillet, PO Box 6025, Dakar, Tel: 21 73 92.

Sierra Leone: Tower Hill, PO Box 124, Freetown, Tel: 22223.

Singapore: 30 Napier Road, Singapore 1025, Tel: 473 1111.

South Africa: 4th floor Federated Building, 38 Ameshoff Street, PO Box 30637, Braamfontein 2017, Johannesburg. Tel: 339 3715. Suite 501, Main Tower, Cape Town Centre, Foreshore, Cape Town 8001. Tel: 4196050.

Soviet Union: British Embassy, Cultural Section, Naberezhnaya Morisa, Toreza 14, Moscow 109072. Tel: 2334507.

Spain: Plaza de Santa Barbara 10, 28004 Madrid. Tel: 419 12 50.

Sri Lanka: 49 Alfred House Gardens, Colombo 3. Tel: 581171.

Sudan: House 60, Street 49, PO Box 1253, Khartoum II East, Tel: 40881.

Sweden: Skarpögatan 6, S-115-27 Stockholm. Tel: 6670 140.

Tanzania: Samora Avenue, PO Box 9100, Dar-es-Salaam. Tel: 22726.

Thailand: British Embassy, BFPO 5, 428 Rama I Road, Siam Square, Bangkok 10500. Tel: 252 6136. 198 Bumrungraj Road, Chiangmai 5000. Tel: 242 103.

Tunisia: British Embassy, BP 229, 5 place de la Victoire, Tunis 1015 RP. Tel: 259 053.

Turkey: Kirlangic Sokak 9, Gazi Osman Pasa, Ankara 06700. Tel: 128 31 65. Cumhuriyet Caddesi 22-24, PK 436, Beyoglu, Ege Han K2, Elmadag, 80074 Istanbul. Tel: 1467125.

Uganda: British High Commission, PO Box 7070, 10/12 Parliament Avenue, Kampala. Tel: 257301.

United Arab Emirates: Al-Jaber Building, 1st floor, Sheik Zayed the First Street, PO Box 248, Abu Dhabi. Tel: 321554. Tariq bin Zaid Street, PO Box 1636, Dubai, Tel: 370 109.

USA: British Embassy, 3100 Massachusetts Avenue NW, Washington DC 20008. Tel: 898 4330.

Venezuela: Torre La Noria, Piso 6, Paseo Enrique Eraso, Sector San Roman, Las Mercedes, Apartado 1246, Caracas 1010A. Tel: 91 52 22.

Yemen Arab Republic: Beit Al-Mottahar, Al-Bonia Street, Harat Handhal, PO Box 2157, Sana'a. Tel: 73179.

Yugoslavia: Generala Zdanova 34-Mezanin, Post Fah 248, 11001 Belgrade. Tel: 332 441.

Zambia Heroes Place, Cairo Road, PO Box 34571, Lusaka. Tel: 214022.

Zimbabwe: 23 Stanley Avenue, PO Box 664, Harare, Tel: 790 627.

Appendix 2
British Organisations for Students from Overseas

The British Refugee Council, Bondway House, 3/9 Bondway, London SW8 1SJ. Tel: (01) 582 6922 (Advice to refugees in Britain, open 9.30am-5.30pm, Monday to Friday, appointments necessary).

International Family Service for Overseas Students, 5th floor, Waterloo House, Waterloo Street, Birmingham B2 5TP. Tel: (021) 643 9539. (Information, advice and practical help for students living in the Birmingham area).

International Society Manchester, 84 Plymouth Grove, Manchester M13 9LW. Tel: (061) 273 1371 (Information on studying and living in the Manchester area, programmes of activities for students).

Joint Council for the Welfare of Immigrants, 115 Old Street, London EC1V 9JR. Tel: (01) 251 8706 (Advice on nationality, immigration and general welfare. Open 10am-1pm and 2pm-6pm, Monday to Friday. Telephone for an appointment).

Leeds Council for Overseas Student Affairs, 155 Woodhouse Lane, Leeds LS2 3ED. Tel: (0532) 460999 (Information on living and studying in the Leeds area).

The National Union of Students (NUS), 461 Holloway Road, London N7 6LJ. Tel: (01) 272 8900 (Information and practical help, welfare issues and students' rights).

The National Union of Students (Northern Ireland), 34 Botanic Avenue, Belfast BT7 1JQ. Tel: (0232) 244641.

The National Union of Students (Scotland), 12 Dublin Street, Edinburgh EH1 3PP. Tel: (031) 556 6598.

Nottingham Area Council for Overseas Student Affairs, 61b Mansfield Road, Nottingham NG1 3PN (Information on studying and living in the Nottingham area).

OSPREY International Student Advisory Council, 4a Bruntsfield Crescent, Edinburgh EH10 4EZ. Tel: (031) 447 9243 (Advice and information for students in Scotland).

Thames Valley Council for Overseas Student Affairs, 1 Beaumont Place, Oxford OX1 2PJ. Tel: (0865) 57236.

United Kingdom Immigrants Advisory Service (UKIAS), 190 Great Dover Street, London SE1 4YB, Tel: (01) 357 6917 (Advice and practical help for people with immigration problems).

UKIAS Refugee Unit, (address as above). Tel: (01) 357 7421.

United Kingdom Council for Overseas Student Affairs (UKCOSA), 60 Westbourne Grove, London W2 5SH. Tel: (01) 229 9268 (Information, advice and practical help, on all matters concerning students from overseas once they have arrived in Britain. Open 10am-12.30pm and 1.00pm-4.00pm, Monday to Friday. Visits by appointment only.

Appendix 3
Government Offices

Department of Education and Science (England and Wales), Elizabeth House, York Road, London SE1 7PH. Tel: (01) 934 9000.

Department of Education for Northern Ireland, Rathgael House, Balloo Road, Bangor, Co. Down BT19 2PR. Tel: (0247) 466311.

The Home Office, Immigration and Nationality Department, Lunar House, Wellesley Road, Croydon CR9 2BY. Tel: (01) 686 0688 (Open 9am–4pm, Monday to Friday).

Local public enquiry offices:

Belfast: Immigration Office, Customs House Square, Belfast BT1 3ET (Open 2pm–4pm, Wednesdays and Thursdays).

Glasgow: Immigration Office, 16 Princes Square, 48 Buchanan Street, Glasgow (Open 9.30am–12.30pm and 2pm–4pm, Monday to Friday).

Harwich: Immigration Office, Parkeston Quay, Harwich (Open 2pm–4pm Monday to Friday).

Liverpool: Immigration Office, Graeme House, Derby Square, Liverpool (Open 2pm–4pm, Tuesday to Friday).

Norwich: Immigration Office, Norwich Airport, Norwich (Open 2.30pm–5pm, Monday to Friday).

Southampton: Immigration Office, Town Quay, Southampton (Open 11am–1pm and 3pm–5pm, Monday to Friday).

Scottish Education Department, Haymarket House, Clifton Terrace, Edinburgh EH12 5DT.

Appendix 4
Professional
Organisations

Accountancy
The Chartered Association of Certified Accountants, 29 Lincoln's Inn Fields, London WC2A 3EE. Tel: (01) 242 6855.

Institute of Chartered Accountants in England and Wales, Chartered Accountants Hall, Moorgate Place, London EC2P 2BJ. Tel: (01) 628 7060.

Institute of Chartered Accountants in Scotland, 27 Queen Street, Edinburgh EH12 1LA. Tel: (031) 225 5673.

Institute of Cost and Management Accountants, 63 Portland Place, London W1N 4AB. Tel: (01) 637 4710.

Agriculture
National Consultative Committee for Agricultural Education, 2 Looms Lane, Bury St Edmunds, Suffolk IP33 1HE.

Air pilots, engineers and navigators
Guild of Air Pilots and Navigators, 30 Eccleston Street, London SW1W 9PY. Tel: (01) 730 0471.

Architecture
Royal Institute of British Architects, 66 Portland Place, London W1N AD. Tel: (01) 580 5533.

Royal Incorporation of Architects in Scotland, 15 Rutland Square, Edinburgh EH1 2BF. Tel: (031) 229 7205.

Banking and insurance
Chartered Insurance Institute, 20 Aldermanbury, London EC2V 7HY. Tel: (01) 606 3835.

Chartered Institute of Bankers, 10 Lombard Street, London EC3 9AR. Tel: (01) 623 3531.

Biology
Institute of Biology, 20 Queensbury Place, London SW7 2DZ. Tel: (01) 581 8333.

Business studies and management
Institute of Chartered Secretaries and Administrators, 16 Park Crescent, London W1N 4AH. Tel: (01) 580 4741.

Institute of Management Services, 1 Cecil Court, London Road, Enfield, Middlesex EN2 6DD. Tel: (01) 363 7452.

Institute of Marketing, Moor Hall, Cookham, Maidenhead, Berkshire SL6 9HQ. Tel: (06285) 24922.

Institute of Personnel Management, 135 Camp Road, London SW19. Tel: (01) 946 9100.

Chemistry
The Royal Society of Chemistry, 30 Russell Square, London WC1 5DP. Tel: (01) 631 1355.

Chiropody
The Society of Chiropodists, 8 Wimpole Street, London W1M 8BX. Tel: (01) 486 3381.

Computer studies
British Computer Society, 13 Mansfield Street, London W1M 0BP. Tel: (01) 637 0471.

Dentists
General Dental Council, 37 Wimpole Street, London WC1R 5DX. Tel: (01) 486 2171.

Doctors
General Medical Council, 44 Hallam Street, London W1N 6AE. Tel: (01) 580 7642.

Engineering
Fellowship of Engineering Institutions, 2 Little Smith Street, London SW1P 3DL. Tel: (01) 799 2688.

Institute of Marine Engineers, 76 Mark Lane, London EC3R 7JN. Tel (01) 481 8493.

Hotel and catering
Hotel Catering and Institutional Management Association, 191 Trinity Road, London SW17 7HN. Tel: (01) 672 4251.

Law
The Law Society (England and Wales), 113 Chancery Lane, London WC2A 1PL. Tel: (01) 242 1222.

The Law Society of Scotland, Law Society's Hall, 26 Drumsburgh Gardens, Edinburgh EH3 7YR.

Council of Legal Education (Ireland), Institute of Professional Legal Studies, Queen's University, Belfast BT7 1NN.

Librarianship
The Library Association, 7 Ridgmount Street, London WC1E 7AE. Tel: (01) 636 7543.

Metallurgy
Institute of Metals, Northway House, High Road, Whetstone, London N20 9LW. Tel: (01) 839 4071.

Physics
The Institute of Physics, 47 Belgrave Square, London SW1X 8QX. Tel: (01) 235 6111.

Physiotherapy
The Chartered Society for Physiotherapy, 14 Bedford Row, London WC1R 4ED. Tel: (01) 242 1941.

Surveying
Royal Institution of Chartered Surveyors, 12 Great George Street, London SW1P 3AD. Tel: (01) 222 7000.

Statistics
The Royal Statistical Society, 25 Enford Street, London W1H 2BH. Tel: (01) 723 5882.

Textiles
The Textile Institute, 10 Blackfriars Street, Manchester M3 5DR. Tel: (061) 834 8457.

Timber technology
Institute of Wood Science, Premier House, 150 Southampton Row, London WC1B 5AL. Tel: (01) 837 8219.

Town planning
Royal Town Planning Institute, 26 Portland Place, London W1N 4BE. Tel: (01) 636 9107.

Transport
Chartered Institute of Transport, 80 Portland Place, London W1N
4DP. Tel: (01) 636 9952.

Veterinary surgeons
Royal College of Veterinary Surgeons, 32 Belgrave Square, London
SW1X 8PQ. Tel: (01) 235 4971.

Appendix 5
Universities and Polytechnics in England and Wales

Bath	Bath University, Claverton Down, Bath BA2 7AY. Tel: (0225) 826826.
Birmingham	The University of Birmingham, PO Box 363, Birmingham B15 2TT. Tel: (021) 414 3344.
	Aston University, Aston Triangle, Birmingham B4 7ET. Tel: (021) 359 6313.
	City of Birmingham Polytechnic, Perry Barr, Birmingham B42 2SU. Tel: (021) 331 5000.
Bradford	The University of Bradford, Bradford, West Yorkshire BD7 1DP. Tel: (0274) 733466.
Brighton	The University of Sussex, Sussex House, Falmer, Brighton BN1 9RH. Tel: (0273) 678416.
	Brighton Polytechnic, Moulsecoomb, Lewes Road, Brighton BN2 4AT. Tel: (0273) 693655.
Bristol	Bristol University, Bristol BS8 1TH. Tel: (0272) 303030.
	Bristol Polytechnic, Coldharbour Lane, Frenchay, Bristol BS16 1QY. Tel: (0272) 656261.
Cambridge	Cambridge University, The Cambridge Inter-collegiate Applications Office, Kellet Lodge, Tennis Court Road, Cambridge CB2 1QJ. Tel: (0223) 333308.
Coventry	Coventry Polytechnic, Priory Street, Coventry CV1 5FB. Tel: (0203) 631313.
Durham	The University of Durham, Old Shire Hall, Durham DH1 3HP. Tel: (091) 374 2000.
East Anglia	The University of East Anglia, Norwich NR4 7TJ. Tel: (0603) 56161.

Essex	The University of Essex, Wivenhoe Park, Colchester CO4 3SQ. Tel: (0206) 873333.
Exeter	Exeter University, Exeter, Devon EX4 4QJ. Tel: (0392) 263263.
Hatfield	Hatfield Polytechnic, College Lane, Hatfield, Hertfordshire AL10 9AB. Tel: (07072) 79000.
Huddersfield	Huddersfield Polytechnic, Queensgate, Huddersfield HD1 3DH. Tel: (0484) 22288.
Hull	The University of Hull, Hull, North Humberside HU6 7RX. Tel: (0482) 46311
Kent	The University of Kent at Canterbury, Canterbury, Kent CT2 7NZ. Tel: (0227) 764000.
Kingston-upon-Thames	Kingston Polytechnic, Kingston Hill, Kingston-upon-Thames KT2 7LB. Tel: (01) 549 1141.
Lancashire	Lancashire Polytechnic, Preston PR1 2TQ. Tel: (0772) 221141.
Lancaster	Lancaster University, Lancaster LA1 4YW. Tel: (0524) 65201.
Leeds	Leeds University, Leeds LS2 9JT. Tel: (0532) 333993.
	Leeds Polytechnic, Calverley Street, Leeds LS1 3HE. Tel: (0532) 462903.
Leicester	Leicester University, Leicester LE1 7RH. Tel: (0533) 522522.
	Leicester Polytechnic, PO Box 143, Leicester LE1 9HB. Tel: (0533) 551551.
Liverpool	Liverpool University, PO Box 147, Liverpool L69 3BX. Tel: (051) 709 6022.
	Liverpool Polytechnic, Rodney House, 70 Mount Pleasant, Liverpool L3 5UX. Tel: (051) 207 3581.
London	Brunel University, The University of West London, Uxbridge, Middlesex UB8 3PH. Tel: (0895) 74000.
	Central London Polytechnic, 309 Regent Street, London W1R 8AL. Tel: (01) 580 2020.
	City of London Polytechnic, 31 Jewry Street, London EC3N 2EY. Tel: (01) 283 1030.
	The City University, Northampton Square, London EC1V 0HB. Tel: (01) 253 4399.

Royal Holloway and Bedford New College, Egham Hill, Egham, Surrey TW20 0EX. Tel: (0784) 34455.

Goldsmith's College, Lewisham Way, London SE14 6NW. Tel: (01) 692 7171.

Imperial College of Science and Technology, South Kensington, London SW7 2AZ. Tel: (01) 589 5111.

King's College, Strand, London WC2R 2LS. Tel: (01) 836 5454.

London School of Economics and Political Science, Houghton Street, London WC2A 2AE. Tel: (01) 405 7686.

Queen Mary College, Mile End Road, London E1 4NS. Tel: (01) 980 4811.

North London Polytechnic, Holloway Road, London N7 8DB. Tel: (01) 607 2789.

North East London Polytechnic, Barking Precinct, Longbridge Road, Dagenham, Essex RM8 2AS. Tel: (01) 590 7722.

Middlesex Polytechnic, Trent Park, Cockfosters Road, Barnet EN4 0PT. Tel: (01) 368 1299.

School of Oriental and African Studies, Malet Street, London WC1E 7HP. Tel: (01) 637 2388.

School of Slavonic and East European Studies, London WC1E 7HU. Tel: (01) 637 4934.

South Bank Polytechnic, Borough Road, London SE1 0AA. Tel: (01) 928 8989.

Thames Polytechnic, Wellington Street, Woolwich, London SE18 6PF. Tel: (01) 854 2030.

University College, Gower Street, London WC1E 6BT. Tel: (01) 387 7050.

Westfield College, Kidderpore Avenue, Hampstead, London NW3 7ST. Tel: (01) 435 7141.

Wye College, Wye, Ashford, Kent TN25 5AH. Tel: (0233) 812401.

Heythrop College, 11-13 Cavendish Square, London W1M 0AN. Tel: (01) 580 6941.

The School of Pharmacy, 29–39 Brunswick Square, London WC1N 1AX. Tel: (01) 837 7651.

Charing Cross and Westminster Medical School, St Dunstan's Road, London W6 8RP. Tel: (01) 748 2040.

King's College School of Medicine and Dentistry, Bessemer Road, London SE5 9PJ. Tel: (01) 274 6222.

The London Hospital Medical College, Turner Street, London E1 2AD. Tel: (01) 377 7611.

Royal Free Hospital School of Medicine, Rowland Hill Street, London NW3 2PF. Tel: (01) 794 0500.

St Bartholomew's Hospital Medical College, West Smithfield, EC1A 7BE. Tel: (01) 606 7404.

St George's Hospital Medical School, Cranmer Terrace, Tooting, London SW17 0RE. Tel: (01) 672 9944.

St Mary's Hospital Medical School, Norfolk Place, Paddington, London W2 1PG. Tel: (01) 723 1252.

United Medical and Dental Schools of Guy's and St Thomas's Hospitals, St Thomas's Hospital, Lambeth Palace Road, London SE1 7EH. Tel: (01) 922 8013.

University College and Middlesex School of Medicine, University College London, Gower Street, London WC1E 6BT. Tel: (01) 387 7050.

University College and Middlesex School of Dentistry, University College London, Gower Street, London WC1E 6BT. Tel: (01) 387 9300.

Loughborough Loughborough University of Technology, Loughborough, Leicestershire LE11 3TU. Tel: (0509) 263171.

Manchester Manchester University, Manchester M13 9PL. Tel: (061) 275 2000.

The University of Manchester Institute of Science and Technology, Manchester M60

1QD. Tel: (061) 236 3311.

Manchester Polytechnic, All Saints, Manchester M15 6BH. Tel: (061) 228 6171.

Newcastle upon Tyne Newcastle upon Tyne University, Newcastle upon Tyne NE1 7RU. Tel: (091) 232 8511.

Newcastle upon Tyne Polytechnic, Ellison Building, Ellison Place, Newcastle upon Tyne NE1 8ST. Tel: (091) 232 6002.

Nottingham The University of Nottingham, University Park, Nottingham NG7 2RD. Tel: (0602) 484848.

Trent Polytechnic, Burton Street, Nottingham NG1 4BU. Tel: (0602) 418248.

Oxford Oxford Colleges Admissions Office, University Offices, Wellington Square, Oxford OX1 2JD. Tel: (0865) 270207.

Oxford Polytechnic, Gipsy Lane, Headington, Oxford OX3 0BP. Tel: (0865) 64777.

Plymouth Polytechnic South West, Drake Circus, Plymouth PL4 8AA. Tel: (0752) 600600.

Portsmouth Portsmouth Polytechnic, Museum Road, Portsmouth PO1 2QQ. Tel: (0705) 827681.

Reading The University of Reading, PO Box 217, Reading RG6 2AH. Tel: (0734) 875123.

Salford The University of Salford, Salford M5 4WT. Tel: (061) 736 5843.

Sheffield The University of Sheffield, Sheffield S10 2TN. Tel: (0742) 768555.

Sheffield City Polytechnic, Pond Street, Sheffield S1 1WB. Tel: (0742) 720911.

Southampton Southampton University, Southampton SO9 5NH. Tel: (0703) 559122.

Staffordshire The University of Keele, Keele, Staffordshire ST5 5BG. Tel: (0782) 621111.

North Staffordshire Polytechnic, College Road, Stoke on Trent ST4 2DE. Tel: (0782) 744531.

Sunderland Sunderland Polytechnic, Langham Tower, Ryhope Road, Sunderland SR2 7EE. Tel: (091) 567 6191.

Surrey The University of Surrey, Guildford, Surrey GU2 5XH. Tel: (0483) 571281.

Teeside Teeside Polytechnic, Borough Road, Middlesborough, Cleveland TS1 3BA. Tel: (0642) 218121.

Wales   Saint David's University College Lampeter, Lampeter, Dyfed SA48 7ED. TEl: (0570) 422351.

University College of North Wales, Bangor, Gwynedd LL57 2DG. Tel: (0248) 351151.

University College of Swansea, Singleton Park, Swansea SA2 8PP. Tel: (0792) 295111.

University College of Wales, Aberystwyth, Dyfed SY23 2AX. Tel: (0970) 623177.

The University of Wales, College of Cardiff, PO Box 68, Cardiff CF1 1XL. Tel: (0222) 874412.

The University of Wales College of Medicine, Heath Park, Cardiff CF4 4XN. Tel: (0222) 755944.

The Polytechnic of Wales, Pontypridd, Mid Glamorgan CF37 1DL. Tel: (0443) 480480.

Warwick   The University of Warwick, Coventry CV4 7AL. Tel: (0203) 523523.

Wolverhampton   The Polytechnic of Wolverhampton, Molineux Street, Wolverhampton WV1 1SB. Tel: (0902) 313000.

York   The University of York, Heslington, York YO1 5DD. Tel: (0904) 430000.

UNIVERSITIES IN SCOTLAND AND NORTHERN IRELAND

Aberdeen   The University of Aberdeen, Aberdeen, Scotland AB9 1FX. Tel: (0224) 273504.

Belfast   The Queen's University of Belfast, University Road, Belfast, Northern Ireland BT7 1NN. Tel: (0232) 245133.

Dundee   Dundee University, Dundee, Scotland DD1 4HN. Tel: (0382) 23181.

Edinburgh   The University of Edinburgh, Edinburgh, Scotland EH8 9YL. Tel: (031) 667 1011.

Herriot-Watt University, Riccarton, Edinburgh, Scotland EH14 4AS. Tel: (031) 449 5111.

Glasgow   The University of Glasgow, Glasgow, Scotland

G12 8QQ. Tel: (041) 339 8855.

The University of Strathclyde, Glasgow, Scotland G1 1XQ. Tel: (041) 552 4400.

St Andrews   The University of St Andrews, College Gate, St Andrews, Scotland KY16 9AJ. Tel: (0334) 76161.

Stirling   Stirling University, Stirling, Scotland FK9 4LA. Tel: (0786) 73171.

Ulster   The University of Ulster, Coleraine, Co. Londonderry, Northern Ireland BT52 1SA. Tel: (0265) 4141.

Appendix 6
Other Useful Addresses

British Tourist Authority, 12 Regent Street, London SW1Y 4PG. Tel: (01) 730 3400.

The Educational Counselling and Credit Transfer Information Service, PO Box 88, Walton Hall, Milton Keynes MK7 6DB. Tel: (0908) 368921 (for information about courses of further and higher education and course entry requirements).

International Students House (ISH), 229 Great Portland Street, London W1N 5HD. Tel: (01) 631 3223 (this is a club for overseas students in London. As well as providing temporary accommodation, ISH can provide you with information about hostel accommodation elsewhere).

Law Centres Federation, Duchess House, 18–19 Warren Street, London W1P 5DB. Tel: (01) 387 8570 (contact this office to find out where your nearest Law Centre is located).

The London Tourist Board, 26 Grosvenor Gardens, London SW1W 0DU. Tel: (01) 730 3488.

The National Association of Citizens Advice Bureaux, Myddleton House, 115/123 Pentonville Road, London N1 6LZ. Tel: (01) 833 2181 (there are citizens advice bureaux in most major towns and cities throughout Britain. The address of your nearest office can be found in the local telephone directory, under 'C').

National Council of YMCAs, 640 Forest Road, London E17 3DZ. Tel: (01) 520 5599.

Northern Ireland Tourist Board, River House, 48 High Street, Belfast BT1 2DS. Tel: (0232) 246609.

Release, 1 Elgin Avenue, London W9 3PR. Tel: (01) 603 8654 (for advice on drugs, arrests and your legal rights).

Scottish Tourist Board, 23 Ravelston Terrace, Edinburgh EH4 3EU. Tel: (031) 332 2433.

SHAC (The London Housing Aid Centre), 189a Old Brompton Road, London SW5 0AR. Tel: (01) 373 7276.

Wales Tourist Board, Brunel House, 2 Fitzalan Road, Cardiff CF2 1UY. Tel: (0222) 499909.

Youth Hostels Association, 14 Southampton Street, London WC2E 7HY. Tel: (01) 836 8541 (for temporary accommodation in Youth Hostels throughout the country).

Young Womens Christian Association of Great Britain, 57 Great Russell Street, London WC1 4AX. Tel: (01) 430 1524.

Glossary

A levels. Examinations usually taken in the sixth year of secondary school, but also open to students of any age whether they are at school, college or studying privately.

Appeal. In the context of immigration control, making an appeal means that a decision made by the immigration authorities is being questioned and will be reconsidered.

Boarding school. Type of school where pupils also live during term time.

British Council. Organisation which promotes Britain and maintains cultural relations overseas, through education, science, technology and the arts.

Citizens Advice Bureau. Place to go for help and advice on a variety of matters including personal, legal, financial and consumer rights.

Co-educational school. School where girls and boys are taught together.

Continuous assessment. Method of examining students where work is assessed throughout the course and marks awarded count towards the final mark.

Dependants. Wife and children under the age of 18.

Deportation. The process of sending a person out of the United Kingdom. Must be by recommendation of a court of law or by order of the Home Secretary.

Entrance requirements. Level of achievement, in terms of examinations passed or experience gained, required before a student can be accepted onto a particular course.

Examination board. Administrative organisation which sets and marks examinations.

Fees. Money paid for a course of tuition or to take an examination.

GCSE. The General Certificate of Secondary Education. An examination usually taken in the fourth or fifth year of secondary school, but can be taken by anyone over the age of 16.

Hall of residence. A large building, usually owned by a college, providing accommodation and, in some cases, meals for students.

Home Office. Government office dealing with the administration and enforcement of immigration regulations.

Illegal entrant. Someone who has entered the United Kingdom without permission to do so, or who has obtained permission by using deception.

Illegal immigrant. Someone who has remained in the United Kingdom beyond the time-limit stamped in their passport and who has not applied for an extension of leave to remain (usually referred to as an overstayer).

Landlord or landlady. If you are renting private accommodation, the landlord is the person who owns this accommodation.

Leave to remain. The time-limit you have on your stay in Britain.

Professional qualification. A qualification which facilitates entry into a certain career.

Professional institution. An association of people working in the same areas, for example banking, accountancy, or law.

Removal. Term used when someone is refused entry to the United Kingdom by the Immigration authorities without reference to a government minister or to a court of law (often confused with deportation). Someone being removed has no right of appeal. The term also refers to the sending away of illegal entrants.

Sandwich course. A type of course which requires the student to spend time away from college gaining practical work experience.

Scholarship. Money paid to a student of merit to enable him/her to follow a further course of education.

Settled status. Status of someone who no longer has a time-limit on their stay in the United Kingdom (means the same as Permanent Residence).

Season ticket. A travel ticket which allows unlimited travel on a certain route within a specified period of time. Usually works out cheaper than buying a separate ticket for each journey.

Sponsorship. Money paid to a student by a potential employer.

Student union. An organisation representing students and their rights.

Syllabus. A published account of subjects covered by a course or an examination.

Thesis. A description of research into a particular topic, usually involving analysis and deduction (sometimes referred to as a dissertation).

Vocational course. A course which provides training for a specific job or career.

Welfare officer. Person employed by a college or student union who specialises in providing advice and practical help to student with problems of any sort, including educational, personal, financial. Sometimes known as Student Services Officer.

Work permit. Evidence, stamped in passport, of having been given permission to take employment.

Yellow pages. Telephone directory with a yellow cover which lists addresses and telephone numbers of local organisations, businesses and services.

Useful Acronyms

A Level	Advanced Level
AA	Automobile Association
ADAR	Art and Design Admissions Registry
ARBS	Association for the Recognition of Business Schools
ARELS-FELCO	Association of Recognised English Language Teaching Establishments
A/S Level	Advanced Supplementary Level
BA	Bachelor of Arts
BA	British Airways
BACIFHE	British Accreditation Council for Independent Further and Higher Education
BASCELT	British Association of State Colleges in English Language Teaching
BBC	British Broadcasting Corporation
BEd	Bachelor of Education
BEng	Bachelor of Engineering
BR	British Rail
BSc	Bachelor of Science
BT	British Telecom
BTA	British Tourist Authority
BTEC	Business and Technician Education Council
BTech	Bachelor of Technology
CAB	Citizens Advice Bureau
CBI	Confederation of British Industry
CGLI	City and Guilds of London Institute
CIFE	Conference for Independent Further Education
CNAA	Council for National Academic Awards
CPE	Cambridge Proficiency Examination
CRAC	Careers Research and Advisory Council
CRCH	Central Register and Clearing House
DE	Department of Employment
DES	Department of Education and Science
DHSS	Department of Health and Social Security
DipHE	Diploma of Higher Education
DSS	Department of Social Security

EAP	English for Academic Purposes
EC	European Community
EEC	European Economic Community
EFL	English as a Foreign Language
ELTS	English Language Testing Service
ESL	English as a Second Language
ESP	English for Special Purposes
FCO	Foreign and Commonwealth Office
FE	Further Education
FO	Foreign Office
GCSE	General Certificate of Secondary Education
GTTR	Graduate Teacher Training Registry
HE	Higher Education
HND	Higher National Diploma
HO	Home Office
IB	International Baccalaureate
ISH	International Students' House
ISIC	International Student Identity Card
ISTA	Independent Secretarial Teaching Association
ITTAC	Information Technology Training Accreditation Council
JMB	Joint Matriculation Board
LCCI	London Chamber of Commerce and Industry
LEA	Local Education Authority
LEAG	London and East Anglian Group
LLB	Bachelor of Laws
MA	Master of Arts
MEG	Midland Examining Group
MOT	Ministry of Transport (Roadworthiness test)
MPhil	Master of Philosophy
MSc	Master of Science
NASTO	National Association of Student Travel Offices
NEA	Northern Examining Group
NHS	National Health Service
NISEC	Northern Ireland Schools Examination Council
NUS	National Union of Students
O Level	Ordinary Level
PCAS	Polytechnics Central Admission System
PEI	Pitman Examination Institute
PhD	Doctor of Philosophy
PO	Post Office
RAC	Royal Automobile Club

RSA	Royal Society of Arts
SCE	Scottish Certificate of Education
SEG	Southern Examining Group
SUCE	Scottish Universities Council on Entrance
UCCA	Universities Central Council on Admissions
UKCOSA	United Kingdom Council for Overseas Student Affairs
UKIAS	United Kingdom Immigration Advisory Service
UNESCO	United Nations Educational, Scientific and Cultural Organisation
WJEC	Welsh Joint Education Committee
YMCA	Young Men's Christian Association
YWCA	Young Women's Christian Association

Index